SYNAPSE OBSERVER

Love & Relationships

Bonds & Connections

Contents

1

Chapter 1: Foundations of Genuine Love

Last year, I attended a wedding that was the talk of the town. It had everything—sparkling decorations, an extravagant venue, and a guest list that could rival the Oscars. But as I watched the bride and groom exchange vows, I noticed something extraordinary. Their eyes were locked, and in that moment, the world around them faded away. The glitzy surroundings seemed to disappear, leaving just the two of them in a bubble of pure connection. It made me realise that love, in its truest form, doesn't need the glitz. Instead, it's about two people sharing a bond that transcends material things.

1.1 The Essence of Love Beyond Material

When we talk about love, what comes to mind? Is it the flowers, the chocolates, or perhaps the grand gestures that we see in movies? While these can be delightful, they often overshadow the real essence of love. Love is an emotional and spiritual connection—a meeting of minds and hearts that goes deeper than anything you can touch or see. It's the feeling of knowing someone truly understands you, the comfort of being accepted for who you are without any pretence. It's like Greek philosopher Aristotle once said, love is "a single soul inhabiting two bodies." This kind of connection can't be bought or wrapped in a box; it's something that grows with every shared moment and whispered secret.

At the heart of any strong relationship is emotional intimacy. It's the core that holds everything together. Think about your closest friendships or family bonds. What's most precious isn't the gifts exchanged but the moments of shared laughter, the shoulder to cry on, and the unspoken understanding. These are the things that create a rich tapestry of memories that outshine any material possession. It's about the spiritual bond between partners that creates a sense of unity and strength that money can't buy. A relationship grounded in emotional intimacy is like a warm blanket on a cold day; it provides comfort, security, and warmth that material things simply can't match.

True love is selfless. It's about putting someone else's happiness above your own, not because you have to, but because you want to. This doesn't mean losing yourself in the process, but rather finding joy in acts of kindness and empathy. Whether it's staying up late to help a friend through a tough time or sacrificing your own comfort to support a loved one's dreams, love is about giving without expecting anything in return. It's those little acts of care—from making a cup of tea when someone is feeling down to simply being there when needed— that truly show love's unselfish nature. These moments may seem small, but they weave a strong fabric of trust and respect that can withstand any challenge.

Love is also an unconditional force. It doesn't keep score or hold grudges. It sees beyond imperfections and embraces flaws. In a world where everything seems to come with conditions, unconditional love stands as a beacon of hope. When you love someone without expecting anything in return, you create a sanctuary where they feel safe to be themselves. It's about accepting each other's quirks, forgiving mistakes, and celebrating individuality. This kind of love doesn't depend on what someone can offer materially; instead, it thrives on emotional support and mutual admiration.

Material fulfillment might provide a momentary thrill, but it's the emotional fulfillment that leaves a lasting impression. Imagine receiving an expensive gift that you cherish for a few days, only to have it lose its shine over time. Now, think about a heartfelt conversation with a loved one that leaves you feeling understood and valued. Which one stays with you longer? Emotional fulfillment enriches your life in ways that material possessions can't. It's the laughter shared over a simple meal, the companionship during a walk in the park, and the comfort of a long hug after a tough day. It's these moments that fill our hearts with warmth and contentment, proving that true fulfillment lies in the connections we nurture, not the things we own.

Reflection Moment: Discover Your Love Language

Take a moment to reflect on how you express love. Is it through words of affirmation, quality time, acts of service, physical touch, or receiving gifts? Understanding your love language can help you deepen your connections and appreciate the different ways love is shared and felt. Consider keeping a journal to note the small acts of love you give and receive each day, and see how they contribute to your emotional fulfillment.

1.2 Emotional Wealth vs. Material Wealth

Picture a treasure chest. What do you imagine inside—glittering jewels, stacks of gold coins, maybe a crown or two? Now, imagine opening that chest and finding it filled not with riches, but with laughter shared over a family dinner, the warmth of a friend's hug, or the comfort of a late-night chat with a loved one. This is emotional wealth. It's the richness that comes from nurturing meaningful relationships and personal connections. It's built on the foundation of emotional support networks and strong family bonds. These are the people who stand by you, who lift you up when you're down, and who celebrate your victories, big or small. Emotional wealth isn't something you can count or measure. It's felt in the heart and seen in the smiles of those you hold dear.

On the flip side, material wealth is like that fleeting thrill you get from a new purchase. Sure, buying that latest gadget or a shiny new pair of shoes can be exciting. But how long does that excitement last? Material possessions provide temporary satisfaction. They can't hug you when you're sad or listen to your dreams and fears. The thrill of acquiring something new quickly fades, leaving you searching for the next thing to fill the void. It's like chasing a shadow—no matter how fast you run, you can never quite catch it.

Consider the lives of some of the wealthiest individuals in the world. Despite their financial success, many report feeling isolated and unfulfilled. They have all the material wealth one could dream of, yet often lack genuine relationships. This highlights a crucial point: material wealth cannot compensate for emotional voids. You can have all the money in the world, but without someone to share it with, it feels hollow. Emotional connections provide the warmth and companionship that money simply can't buy.

So why do we often prioritise material wealth over emotional wealth? Society frequently tells us that success is measured by what we have rather than who we are or who we connect with. But think about the moments that bring you true joy. Is it the new car, or is it the road trip with friends where you laughed until your sides hurt? Is it the designer outfit, or is it the compliment from a stranger that made you feel truly seen? Emotional wealth offers a richness that material wealth can never match. It's about finding joy and fulfillment in the connections we build, not the things we accumulate.

Reflection Prompt: Assess Your Emotional Bank Account

Take a moment to reflect on your own emotional wealth. Who are the people in your life that contribute to it? Consider making a list of the relationships that bring you joy and support. How often do you invest time and energy into these connections compared to your pursuit of material possessions? Reflect on ways you might prioritise nurturing these relationships, just as you would your financial savings.

1.3 Authenticity in Relationships: A Core Principle

Let's talk authenticity. Imagine peeling away layers of an onion. Each layer reveals more of what's inside, much like authenticity in relationships. It's about being true to who you are and allowing others to see that. In relationships, authenticity is the bedrock of trust and intimacy. When you're genuine, you're letting others see your true self, quirks and all. It's like going out without makeup—not because you have to, but because you feel comfortable enough to show your natural self. Authenticity invites others to drop their masks too, creating a safe space where real connections flourish.

Consider the last time you had an honest conversation with someone. Not the kind where you nod and smile politely, but one where you dive deep into your fears and dreams. Maybe it was with a friend over coffee, where you admitted your anxiety about the future or shared a long-held aspiration. This type of dialogue opens doors to deeper understanding. It's like shining a flashlight into a dark room, illuminating parts of yourself that you usually keep hidden. Such vulnerability, far from being a weakness, becomes a strength in relationships. It builds bridges of empathy and compassion, fostering a sense of solidarity and support.

Yet, the path to authenticity isn't always smooth. Fear of judgement or rejection can create barriers. We worry about how others perceive us, often hiding our true selves behind facades. It's like wearing a heavy coat in summer—uncomfortable and unnecessary. These fears can prevent us from expressing our genuine thoughts and feelings, trapping us in superficial interactions. Overcoming these barriers requires courage. It means embracing the belief that you are worthy of love and acceptance just as you are. This is easier said than done, but acknowledging these fears is the first step toward breaking free from them.

So, how does one cultivate authenticity? Start with open communication. Share your thoughts honestly, even when it's scary. This might mean telling your partner how you really feel about an issue rather than brushing it off. Self-reflection is another powerful tool. Spend time understanding your own values and beliefs. Journaling can help. Write down your thoughts and emotions. It's like having a conversation with yourself, peeling back the layers to see what's underneath. The more you practise this, the more natural it will become to express your authentic self in your relationships.

Reflection Exercise: Unmasking Your Authentic Self

Take a moment to reflect on a recent interaction where you felt truly authentic. What was it about that situation that allowed you to be yourself? Write about it. Now, think about a time when you didn't feel authentic. What held you back? Consider ways you can bring more authenticity into your daily interactions. This could be as simple as sharing your opinion in a group discussion or expressing gratitude to someone who made a difference in your day.

Authenticity in relationships doesn't mean airing every thought or emotion without a filter. It's about knowing when and how to share in a way that honours both yourself and the relationship. Like a dance, it requires rhythm and balance. As you practise authenticity, you'll find that it not only strengthens your connections but also enriches your own understanding of yourself. Embrace it, and watch as your relationships transform into something truly genuine and fulfilling.

1.4 Recognizing True Affection in Everyday Gestures

When was the last time someone cooked you your favourite meal just because? There's something magical about such a simple act. It goes beyond the ingredients and the recipe; it's about the thought and the care that went into it. Preparing a meal for someone is like saying, "I see you, I know what you love, and I want to make you happy." It's funny how a dish of spaghetti can say so much without uttering a word. It's the little things that often speak the loudest, and these small gestures are what truly make us feel cherished. A handwritten note tucked into a lunchbox or slipped under a pillow carries a similar weight. It doesn't have to be a sonnet. A simple "thinking of you" can brighten a day and create a lasting impression.

Being present with someone is one of the greatest gifts you can give. It's a bit like when you're talking to a friend, and suddenly, you realise they've put away their phone, their eyes are on you, and you have their full attention. That's rare these days, isn't it? Everyone's glued to a screen, half-listening while scrolling through their feeds. But when you actively listen, you're telling the person that they matter more than anything else happening at that moment. This kind of focus is invaluable and forms the bedrock of strong relationships. Quality time without distractions, whether it's a quiet evening walk or just sitting together in silence, can speak volumes. It's about being there, truly being there, in a way that no gift can replace.

Acts of service, like helping with daily chores, might not seem like the stuff of romance novels, but they're powerful expressions of love. Imagine coming home to find the laundry done, or the dishes put away. It's like a warm hug after a long day. These acts show commitment and thoughtfulness, reinforcing the sense of partnership and teamwork. Supporting someone's personal goals or ambitions works in the same way. It's standing beside them, cheering them on, helping them reach for the stars. These actions reflect a deep-seated care that transcends any material gift.

Love doesn't always come wrapped in a bow. It's often found in the simplest of gestures and the smallest of things. Love is in the way someone saves you the last cookie or remembers to record your favourite show. It's in the spontaneous dance in the kitchen or the impromptu karaoke session in the car. These non-material expressions of love are what fill our days with joy and laughter. They're the moments that remind us that we are loved for who we are, not for what we have or what we can give in return.

Interactive Element: Create a Gratitude Jar

Consider starting a gratitude jar in your home. Whenever someone does something kind or makes you feel loved, jot it down on a slip of paper and add it to the jar. Encourage others to do the same. Over time, you'll have a collection of small gestures that remind you of the love that surrounds you. On a rainy day, or when you need a reminder of the good, open the jar, and read a few. It's a simple practice that highlights the power of everyday gestures and keeps the focus on what truly matters.

1.5 The Role of Self-Worth in Love

Self-worth is a bit like the roots of a tree. It anchors you, provides strength, and supports your growth. At its core, self-worth is the belief in your inherent value and dignity as a person.

It's about recognizing that you are deserving of love, respect, and happiness simply because you exist. This internal belief is crucial for forming healthy relationships, as it sets the standard for how you allow others to treat you. When you appreciate your own value, you communicate to the world that you deserve to be treated well. It's the foundation upon which every meaningful relationship is built, allowing you to engage with others from a place of confidence and strength rather than insecurity or fear.

Unfortunately, many of us know the feeling of low self-worth all too well. It can sneak up on you, like that unwelcome guest who shows up unannounced. This lack of self-value often leads to seeking validation through material means, like gifts and possessions. You might find yourself craving that new bag or the latest gadget, not because you need it, but because you hope it will fill a gap or prove your worth to others. The harsh reality is, no amount of material wealth can truly compensate for a lack of self-worth. Seeking approval through possessions is like trying to fill a sieve with water—no matter how much you pour in, it just keeps slipping through. This dependency on external validation can lead to unhealthy relationships, where love is conditional on what you can provide materially, rather than who you are.

Building self-worth is not an overnight project. It's a continuous effort, a bit like tending to a garden. You have to nurture it, water it regularly with self-care and positive self-talk. Practising gratitude is a great place to start. It shifts your focus from what you lack to what you have, and it can significantly boost your mood and outlook. Each day, take a moment to acknowledge the things you appreciate about yourself and your life. It might be as simple as being thankful for your morning coffee or recognizing your ability to listen to a friend. Setting personal boundaries is another powerful tool in this toolkit. Boundaries aren't walls to keep people out; they're guidelines for ensuring your needs are respected and met. By clearly defining what is acceptable to you, you teach others how to treat you and affirm your self-worth.

When you nurture self-worth, something beautiful happens: your relationships transform. As you begin to see your own value, you naturally attract relationships that reflect this understanding. You engage with others more authentically, and your love becomes stronger and more genuine. Instead of clinging to relationships out of fear of being alone, you choose them because they enrich your life. This doesn't mean you won't face challenges, but you'll approach them with a mindset rooted in confidence and self-respect. Healthy love flourishes when both parties see and appreciate their own worth and that of their partner. It's an ongoing dance of mutual respect and admiration, where both individuals grow and thrive together.

At the end of the day, self-worth isn't just a nice-to-have; it's an integral part of living a fulfilling life. It colours the way you see the world, impacts your decisions, and shapes your relationships. As you cultivate this inner belief, you open the door to a life of deeper connections and authentic love—one that isn't reliant on material trappings but is rich in emotional depth and understanding.

2

Chapter 2: Navigating Societal Expectations

When I was in high school, there was this unwritten rule about prom: the bigger the limo, the better the night. Everyone wanted to outdo each other, as if the size of your ride determined the quality of your experience. My best friend and I decided to buck the trend. We showed up in her mom's old, slightly rusty sedan, and honestly, we laughed the entire way there. No flashy entrance, just us, singing off-key to the radio. That night, I realised something profound—it wasn't about the car; it was about the company and the memories. This story sets the stage for a critical discussion on societal expectations, especially how they pressure us to equate love and success with material wealth.

In today's world, the pressure to conform to material standards is immense. Social media plays a significant role in shaping our perceptions of love and success. You scroll through your feed and see influencers showcasing their luxurious lifestyles, making it seem like happiness is directly proportional to the number of designer handbags you own. This culture of comparison can lead to a distorted view of what's important. According to the Media Dependency Theory, the more you depend on media, the stronger its influence over your behaviour and perception becomes. By constantly consuming these curated images, you might start equating wealth with love, thinking that without the latest gadgets or trends, you're somehow lacking.

Cultural narratives also contribute to this mindset, promoting the idea that wealth equals love. Think about the fairy tales where the prince showers the princess with jewels or the rom-coms where grand gestures are seen as the ultimate expression of love. These stories seep into our consciousness, making us believe that material possessions are essential for a fulfilling relationship. But what about the emotional strain this places on relationships? When you start measuring love through material means, it creates unrealistic expectations. The pressure to continuously prove your affection with gifts can lead to financial strain, causing stress and resentment. You might find yourself questioning your self-worth, wondering if you're enough without the trappings of wealth.

So, how do we redefine success beyond material possessions? It's about shifting the focus to emotional fulfillment. True success is found in the quality of your relationships and the joy you derive from them. It's about those moments when you feel genuinely seen and appreciated, not the price tag of the gifts exchanged. Emotional wealth should be the metric by which you measure success, not the latest phone model or the number of zeroes in your bank account. This perspective shift can liberate you from the cycle of material validation, allowing you to cultivate deeper, more meaningful connections.

Breaking free from societal pressures isn't always easy, but it is possible. One effective strategy is practising mindful consumption. Before making a purchase, ask yourself: "Do

I really need this, or am I buying it to impress others?" This simple question can help you make more intentional choices, reducing impulse buying and fostering financial security. Another approach is engaging in values-based decision-making. Reflect on your core values and let them guide your actions. If a decision doesn't align with your values, it might be worth reconsidering. By choosing authenticity over conformity, you empower yourself to live a life that truly resonates with who you are.

Interactive Element: Values Clarification Exercise

Take a moment to write down your top five core values. Consider how these values influence your decisions and relationships. Next time you face a choice, refer back to this list. Does the decision align with your values? If not, what adjustments can you make? This exercise can serve as a compass, guiding you toward a more fulfilling, value-driven life.

2.2 The Courage to Defy Societal Norms

Growing up, you might have heard that to be successful, you need to follow a certain path, like climbing a corporate ladder or acquiring specific status symbols. These are the societal norms that often go unquestioned, shaping our beliefs about happiness and love. But here's the thing—questioning these norms is crucial. Why should you accept someone else's definition of happiness without evaluating its relevance to your own life? Critical thinking is your ally here. By analysing media messages, you can start to see the subtle ways they influence you. Advertisements and TV shows frequently equate love with expensive gifts or lavish vacations. It's easy to get swept up in these narratives, but pausing to question them can open your mind to new possibilities and perspectives.

Consider the stories of people who have successfully challenged these norms. Take, for example, a couple I know who decided to forgo a traditional wedding. Instead of spending thousands on a single day, they chose to travel the world together. They prioritised experiences and the memories they would create over possessions that would eventually gather dust. Their choice was an act of defiance, not just against societal expectations, but also against the belief that love is measured by material displays. Their journey taught them the joy of meaningful connections and the richness of shared experiences. Similarly, prioritising genuine relationships over superficial connections can be liberating. The rewards are immense, providing a sense of personal freedom that allows you to live authentically.

When you defy societal norms, you gain enhanced personal freedom. You no longer feel confined by what others expect of you, enabling you to make choices that align with your true values. This freedom extends to your relationships, where the focus shifts from external validation to genuine emotional fulfillment. Imagine not worrying about keeping up with the Joneses, and instead, investing in what genuinely makes you happy. This shift not only strengthens your connections with others but also reinforces your self-worth. You begin to realise that your value isn't tied to material possessions but to the richness of your experiences and the depth of your relationships.

To aid you in this journey of non-conformity, there are various resources and tools available. Consider joining community support groups where you can connect with like-minded individuals who share your desire for authenticity. These groups can offer encouragement and insights from people who have walked the path you're considering. Additionally, inspirational literature and media can provide motivation and guidance. Books and documentaries about minimalism or biographies of individuals who have chosen alternative lifestyles can inspire you to embrace a life that aligns with your true self.

Reflection Section: Evaluate Your Influences

Take a few moments to jot down the societal norms that you feel pressured to conform to. Reflect on which of these align with your personal values and which ones don't. Consider how these norms impact your decisions and relationships. Are there areas where you might want to make a change? Identifying the norms that no longer serve you is the first step toward living a life that's truly your own.

2.3 Embracing Individuality in a Conformist World

When you hear the word "individuality," what comes to mind? Is it standing out in a crowd, being the only one in a sea of sameness? At its core, individuality means embracing who you truly are, especially within the context of love and relationships. It's about recognizing and celebrating your unique traits, quirks, and perspectives. Imagine being in a relationship where you feel free to express yourself without fear of judgement. This is what individuality offers—a space to be authentic, to share your true self with someone who appreciates you for exactly who you are.

I once knew a couple who embodied this beautifully. They were both artists, and their home was a canvas of their lives.

Each room was filled with their own creations, telling stories only they could tell. They wore clothes that reflected their personalities, often mixing colours and patterns in ways that were uniquely theirs. Their individuality shone through their creative self-expression, enhancing their bond and making their partnership vibrant and alive. Instead of merging into one, they celebrated their distinct personalities, proving you don't have to lose yourself to be in a relationship. Their personal styles were a reflection of their inner selves, and they wore their authenticity with pride.

But embracing individuality isn't always a walk in the park. It can feel like swimming against the tide, especially when societal norms push conformity at every corner. The fear of social rejection is real. You might worry about being seen as too different or not fitting in. This fear can be paralysing, discouraging you from expressing your true self. It's like being a chameleon, constantly changing colours to blend in rather than standing out as a vibrant butterfly. The pressure to conform can be overwhelming, leading to self-doubt and a loss of identity. Yet, it's crucial to remember that these challenges are often rooted in the fear of the unknown, not in reality.

So how do you celebrate your individuality in a world that often values sameness? Start by setting personal goals that align with your values. Know what you stand for and what you want to achieve in your life and relationships. This clarity will guide your choices and help you stay true to yourself. Surround yourself with a supportive network of like-minded individuals who appreciate your uniqueness. These are the friends who cheer for you when you succeed and lift you up when you falter. They understand that your quirks are not flaws but essential parts of who you are.

Consider joining communities or groups where individuality is celebrated and nurtured. Whether it's an art class, a book club, or a hiking group, find spaces where you can explore your interests and passions. These environments foster creativity and authenticity, encouraging you to embrace your true self. Engaging in activities that you love not only boosts your self-esteem but also attracts people who appreciate your individuality. This creates a ripple effect, inspiring others to embrace their uniqueness too.

Being yourself in a conformist world takes courage, but it's worth it. The freedom that comes from living authentically is unmatched. It's like taking a deep breath after holding it in for too long—a relief and a revelation. When you honour your individuality, you attract relationships that are grounded in truth and acceptance. You draw people who see you for who you truly are, not who you think you should be. This authenticity strengthens your connections, allowing love to flourish in its purest form. Embracing individuality is not just about standing out; it's about standing firm in your truth, knowing that you are enough just as you are.

The Power of Independent Love

In the world of relationships, independent love is a bit like having your cake and eating it too. It's about maintaining your individuality while being part of something bigger. Loving independently means you don't rely on material validation to feel secure or valued in your relationship. Instead, it's a deep-seated confidence in yourself and your partner, knowing that your love isn't tied to things but to shared experiences and mutual respect. This approach allows both partners to stand strong on their own, creating a relationship where two whole individuals come together to form a powerful bond.

When you practise independent love, you'll notice a boost in your self-confidence. You're not constantly seeking approval or reassurance through gifts or grand gestures. Instead, you understand your worth and recognize that love, at its core, is about connection and understanding. This self-assuredness spills over into your relationship, making it more resilient. You're not clinging to each other out of insecurity, but embracing each other's strengths and supporting each other's growth. This creates a stronger foundation, one that can weather the ups and downs of life. It's like building a house on solid rock rather than shifting sand.

Consider the couple who spends their weekends pursuing separate hobbies—one might be hiking solo, while the other takes a pottery class. They're not drifting apart; they're nurturing their interests and, in turn, bringing fresh energy into the relationship. They prioritise personal growth, not because they need space from each other, but because they understand that being fulfilled individually leads to a more vibrant partnership. This kind of love isn't about losing yourself in another person; it's about finding joy in your own life and sharing that joy with someone you love. It's a dance of togetherness and independence, where both partners have the freedom to grow without losing sight of each other.

To cultivate this independence, start by diving into personal hobbies and interests. Whether it's painting, yoga, or learning a new language, having something that you can call your own is empowering. It not only enriches your life but also gives you something exciting to share with your partner. It adds layers to your relationship, keeping it dynamic and interesting.

Additionally, financial literacy and independence are crucial. Understanding your finances and having a sense of control over them allows you to make decisions based on what truly matters to you, not out of necessity or obligation. It relieves the pressure to rely on someone else for financial security and lets you meet your partner on equal footing.

This independence doesn't mean you don't care about your partner or the relationship. On the contrary, it shows a deep respect for both. It means you're confident enough in your love to let it breathe, to let it grow without suffocating it with constant demands for validation. You trust in the strength of your bond and recognize that love is not about possession but about partnership. It's about walking side by side, not one behind the other, and supporting each other's dreams and aspirations. Independent love is powerful because it acknowledges that while you are two individuals, together, you create something extraordinary.

2.5 Finding Role Models of Non-Materialistic Love

In a world where material wealth often overshadows the simple joys of love, finding role models who embody non-materialistic love can feel like searching for a needle in a haystack. However, these individuals do exist. They are characterised by compassion and empathy, qualities that allow them to connect with others on a profound level. Their love isn't about what they can give materially, but about their willingness to understand and support those they care about. Integrity and authenticity shine through in their actions and words. They remain true to themselves and their partners, allowing relationships to flourish naturally without the pressure of meeting societal expectations.

Consider public figures known for their simplicity. Celebrities who choose a modest lifestyle often capture our attention not just because of their fame, but because they remind us that love and happiness aren't tied to material possessions. Think of authors and thought leaders who write about living a life enriched by experiences rather than things. They inspire us to focus on what truly matters—connections, kindness, and shared moments. These individuals show us that it's possible to live a life filled with love and joy without relying on material wealth to define it. Their stories are like a warm blanket on a chilly day, offering comfort and a reminder that love is about being present and authentic.

Finding such role models can be incredibly empowering. It starts with seeking out inspiring social media accounts that promote minimalist lifestyles and genuine connections. Follow influencers and creators who share their journey of living simply yet meaningfully. These accounts can provide a daily dose of inspiration and remind you that true happiness often comes from within. Community groups focused on minimalist living can also be a valuable resource. Joining these groups allows you to connect with others who share your values, providing support and encouragement as you seek to redefine what love and success mean to you. It's like finding your tribe, a group of individuals who cheer for you as you choose to live authentically.

The impact of having such role models in your life can be transformative. They influence your personal beliefs and actions, encouraging you to prioritise emotional connections over material possessions. As you learn from their experiences and stories, you begin to see the world through a different lens. You might find yourself making more intentional choices, valuing moments over things, and seeking joy in the simplicity of everyday life. This shift not only enriches your relationships but also enhances your overall well-being. It's like discovering a new path that leads to a deeper understanding of love and happiness.

As you embrace these lessons and apply them to your life, you create a ripple effect. Your actions inspire others around you to consider the value of non-materialistic love. You become a role model yourself, showing friends and family that love isn't about what you can give or receive in material terms, but about the genuine connections you cultivate. This isn't just a shift in perspective; it's a change in how you live and love. It's about realising that the true essence of love lies in the moments that make your heart full, not the things that fill your home.

The journey we're on is one of discovery and growth. As we explore the various aspects of love and relationships, we uncover the beauty of emotional connections and the joy that comes from living authentically. Each chapter builds on the last, creating a tapestry of insights and experiences that guide us toward a deeper understanding of what it means to love and be loved. The next chapter delves into the heart of emotional connections, exploring how we can nurture and strengthen these bonds to create relationships that stand the test of time.

3

Chapter 3: Emotional Connections in Relationships

Let me take you back to a moment that changed the way I view relationships. Picture this: a cosy living room, dimly lit, with two friends sitting across from each other. One is sharing a deeply personal story, eyes welling with tears, while the other listens intently, nodding and offering gentle words of support. It was like watching an invisible thread weave them closer together, creating a bond that transcended mere friendship. This scene was a masterclass in emotional intimacy, a concept that forms the bedrock of meaningful relationships. It's that deep-seated connection where you feel truly seen and heard, a place where you can express your most vulnerable self without fear of judgement.

Building emotional intimacy is like constructing a bridge, one plank at a time, each step bringing you closer to another person. It starts with sharing personal stories and experiences. Imagine sitting with someone and peeling back the layers of your life's onion, revealing not just the shiny, happy moments, but also the messy, complicated ones. This sharing isn't about oversharing or dumping your life story in one go. It's about gradually opening up, allowing the other person to walk alongside you through your past, present, and dreams for the future. This kind of sharing fosters a sense of mutual understanding and respect, laying the groundwork for a relationship that is both deep and enduring.

Another way to nurture this intimacy is through regularly expressing gratitude and appreciation. It's like watering a plant; these small acts of kindness and acknowledgment help your relationship grow and flourish. Consider starting each day by telling your partner or friend something you appreciate about them. It could be as simple as thanking them for listening to you vent about your day or appreciating their quirky humour that never fails to make you smile. This practice not only strengthens your bond but also fosters a positive environment where both parties feel valued and cherished.

Trust is the glue that holds emotional intimacy together. Without it, the bridge you build might crumble at the slightest tremor. Trust is earned through consistency in words and actions. It's about showing up for someone, being reliable, and following through on promises. When you say you'll be there, be there. When you promise to listen, listen with an open heart. This consistency helps build a safe space where both of you can express your true selves without the fear of being let down or betrayed. Trust is like a bank account; you deposit small acts of reliability and integrity, and over time, it grows into a robust foundation that can support the weight of any relationship.

However, building emotional intimacy isn't always a walk in the park. Fear of vulnerability is a common barrier that can prevent you from opening up fully. It's that little voice in your head that whispers, "What if they don't like the real me?" But vulnerability is not a weakness; it's a strength that allows you to connect deeply with others. Acknowledge this fear and take small steps to overcome it. Start by sharing a little more than usual, testing the waters before diving in completely. Another challenge might be past relationship traumas that cast long shadows over new connections. These experiences can make you wary, but recognizing them is the first step toward healing. Consider talking to a counsellor or therapist who can help you navigate these feelings and build healthier, more fulfilling relationships.

Reflection Exercise: Intimacy Inventory

Take a moment to reflect on your relationships. Choose one where you'd like to build more emotional intimacy. Write down three personal stories or experiences you could share with this person, and three things you appreciate about them. Over the next week, find opportunities to share these with them. Notice how these exchanges affect your connection and how they make you feel. This small exercise can be a powerful step toward deepening your emotional bonds.

3.2 Communicating Feelings Without Words

Think back to a time when someone caught your eye from across a room. No words were exchanged, yet a smile or a nod communicated volumes. This is the magic of nonverbal communication. It's the silent language of gestures, expressions, and touches that convey emotions and intentions without uttering a single word. Nonverbal cues are like the punctuation marks of our interactions, adding nuance and depth to the sentences we speak. They guide us in understanding the emotions bubbling beneath the surface, helping us connect on a deeper level. The way someone holds their hands, the tilt of their head, or even the rhythm of their breathing can tell you more than an entire conversation.

Body language is one of the most powerful tools in this silent dialogue. Imagine a friend walking toward you with open arms. Just that gesture can signal warmth and welcome, inviting you into their space. Crossed arms, on the other hand, might suggest defensiveness or discomfort. It's like reading a book without words, where each movement tells part of the story. Then there's eye contact, which can be as intimate as a whispered secret. Locking eyes with someone can create a bond stronger than any spoken word. It's a way of saying, "I'm here, I'm present, and I'm listening." Add to that the subtle shifts in facial expressions—an arched eyebrow, a soft smile—and you've got a rich tapestry of communication that goes beyond words.

Physical touch and proximity also play a significant role. A gentle touch on the shoulder can be incredibly reassuring during tough times. It's like a nonverbal "I'm here for you." Imagine sitting next to someone you care about, close enough that your shoulders touch. That proximity can create a sense of closeness and safety. It's a reminder of your connection, even in silence. These forms of nonverbal expression are the unsung heroes of effective communication. They bridge gaps that words sometimes can't cross, making them invaluable in building and maintaining emotional connections.

Practical examples of nonverbal communication abound in everyday life. Picture a parent comforting a child after a fall with a hug that says, "You're safe now." Or imagine sharing a knowing smile with a friend across a bustling café, a silent acknowledgment of an inside joke. These moments highlight the power of nonverbal cues to convey empathy, understanding, and support. They strengthen bonds and make us feel connected, even in a room full of strangers. Nonverbal communication transcends language barriers, allowing us to reach out and touch someone's heart without uttering a single word.

To make the most of nonverbal cues, mindfulness is key. Start by practising mirror exercises to become more aware of your own body language. Spend a few minutes each day observing yourself in the mirror as you speak or react to different scenarios. Notice how your expressions change, how your posture shifts. This awareness helps you understand what you're communicating nonverbally and how others might perceive it. Being intentional about your nonverbal cues can transform your interactions, making them more genuine and effective. It's about tuning in to the unspoken conversation happening beneath the surface and using it to enrich your relationships.

3.3 The Art of Listening: Beyond Hearing

Imagine a conversation where you feel completely understood, where every word you say seems to land perfectly with the person across from you. That's the magic of active listening. It's not just about letting words wash over you; it's about diving deep into what someone is saying, with full engagement and presence. Active listening transforms ordinary exchanges into meaningful connections, where both people feel truly valued. It involves more than just hearing words—it's about connecting with the emotions and intentions behind them. This dynamic process requires your full attention and an open heart, creating a space where genuine understanding can flourish.

It's easy to confuse hearing with listening. Hearing is a passive act, simply receiving sound without much effort. You might hear the hum of traffic, the chatter in a café, or even someone speaking, but listening takes it a step further. It involves actively engaging with the message being conveyed, processing it, and responding thoughtfully. Imagine your friend is sharing a challenging experience, and you nod absently, caught up in your thoughts. You're hearing them, sure, but not truly listening. Contrast this with sitting forward, maintaining an attentive posture, making eye contact, and offering reflective responses that show you're tuned in. This approach confirms your understanding and lets the speaker know you're genuinely invested in what they're saying.

Improving your listening skills is a game-changer for relationships, and it starts with a few simple strategies. First, practise the art of not interrupting. It can be tempting to jump in with your thoughts or solutions, but holding back allows the other person to fully express themselves. Letting them finish shows respect and patience, encouraging deeper sharing. Another tip is to ask open-ended questions, the kind that invite more than a yes or no answer. Questions like "How did that make you feel?" or "What are you thinking about?" encourage the other person to expand on their thoughts, providing richer insights into their feelings and experiences. This openness fosters a deeper connection, as it shows your willingness to understand them fully.

The benefits of being truly heard in a relationship are profound. When someone listens to you with genuine interest, it builds trust and respect. You feel acknowledged and appreciated, knowing your words have weight and meaning. This validation strengthens the bond between you, creating a foundation of mutual respect. Over time, this leads to a deeper emotional connection, where both parties feel safe to express themselves openly. Trust grows, and with it, the relationship thrives. It's like watering a plant consistently, allowing it to grow strong and vibrant. In this nurturing environment, emotional intimacy blossoms, enriching the relationship beyond measure.

Feeling heard also has a ripple effect. It boosts your confidence, reinforcing your self-worth and encouraging you to communicate more openly. Knowing your thoughts and feelings are valued creates a sense of belonging, a reassurance that you matter. This sense of security empowers you to be more authentic, fostering a relationship where both individuals can grow and evolve together. As you practise active listening, you'll notice the positive impact it has on your connections. Conversations become more meaningful, conflicts are resolved more peacefully, and understanding deepens, creating a beautiful tapestry of shared experiences and growth.

Active listening is a skill that can transform your relationships and enrich your life. It's about being present, attentive, and genuinely interested in what others have to say. By cultivating this skill, you open the door to deeper connections, where trust, respect, and understanding flourish.

Emotional Vulnerability: Strength in Openness

In a world that often celebrates stoicism and self-reliance, vulnerability can seem like a weakness. It's that moment when you lay your heart bare, a little uncertain, maybe even a bit wobbly. But here's the truth: vulnerability is a form of courage that opens doors to deeper understanding and connection. It's the ability to show your true self—the raw, unfiltered version—

without the fear of being judged or dismissed. By stepping into this space, you reveal your humanity, inviting others to do the same. Vulnerability becomes a bridge, connecting hearts in ways that mere words can't. It's not about exposing yourself recklessly but rather choosing to be open, even when it's scary. This openness is a powerful strength, one that can enrich your relationships beyond measure.

Being open and vulnerable can profoundly enhance your relationships and personal growth. When you dare to show your true emotions, you create an environment where others feel safe to do the same. This mutual exchange fosters deeper connections, where both parties can truly see and understand each other. Imagine the warmth of knowing someone sees your insecurities and stands by you nonetheless. Emotional openness encourages empathy, as it allows you to step into each other's shoes and experience life from different perspectives. This understanding is the bedrock of strong relationships, creating a sanctuary where both partners can grow and evolve together. As you become more comfortable with vulnerability, you also grow more accepting of yourself. You learn to embrace your imperfections, realising that they are part of what makes you beautifully human.

Of course, the thought of being vulnerable can be daunting. Many of us harbour fears of judgement or rejection, imagining the worst-case scenarios where our openness is met with ridicule or dismissal. It's like standing on the edge of a cliff, looking down into the unknown. These fears are common, but they don't have to hold you back. The key is to acknowledge these feelings and understand that vulnerability is a choice, not a compulsion. You get to decide when and with whom to share your inner world. Start by taking small steps, gradually increasing your comfort level with being open. Perhaps begin with a friend or loved one who has shown themselves to be trustworthy and understanding. As you experience positive responses, your fears will start to dissipate, making room for more genuine connections.

Real-life examples of vulnerability can illuminate its transformative power in relationships. Take the story of Sarah and Alex. Sarah spent years concealing her anxiety, fearing that admitting it would make her seem weak. But when she finally shared her struggles with Alex, she found not judgement but compassion. Alex, in turn, opened up about his own insecurities, which he had kept hidden for fear of seeming inadequate. This exchange of vulnerabilities deepened their bond, allowing them to support each other in ways they hadn't before. Admitting mistakes is another form of vulnerability that can strengthen relationships. It requires humility and the courage to accept responsibility. When you acknowledge a mistake and express a desire to learn from it, you show maturity and respect for the relationship. This honesty fosters trust and demonstrates your commitment to growth, both personally and as a partner.

Vulnerability is not about spilling your guts to anyone who will listen. It's about choosing intentional openness in safe and supportive environments. The more you practice, the more you realize that vulnerability is not a chink in your armor but a powerful tool for connection and growth. It becomes a source of strength, allowing you to build relationships that are both deep and meaningful. Embrace it, and watch as your connections transform into something truly extraordinary.

Nurturing Emotional Bonds Over Time

Picture a garden in spring, blooming with life and colour. Relationships, much like gardens, require ongoing care and attention to flourish. Without it, they risk withering and growing stale. Maintaining emotional connections is a bit like tending to that garden. It's about recognizing the need for consistent effort to keep the relationship vibrant and alive. Complacency can sneak in, especially in long-term relationships, where routines become habits and habits become ruts. To prevent stagnation, it's crucial to actively nurture emotional bonds, ensuring they remain strong and resilient.

One powerful way to keep relationships vibrant is through regular date nights or shared activities. These moments act as reset buttons, pulling you out of the day-to-day grind and into a space where you can focus on each other. It doesn't have to be extravagant—a simple walk in the park or a cosy movie night can work wonders. The key is to be present and engaged, allowing yourselves to reconnect and rediscover the joy of each other's company. Celebrating milestones and achievements is equally important. Whether it's a work promotion, a personal goal met, or even just surviving a hectic week, acknowledging these moments together reinforces your bond and creates shared memories to cherish.

Long-term relationships, however, come with their own set of challenges. Balancing personal growth with the needs of the relationship can be tricky. It's like walking a tightrope, trying to move forward without losing balance. Both partners need space to grow individually, yet must also invest in growing together. This balance can foster a dynamic where both parties are fulfilled and motivated to support each other's ambitions. Over time, external stressors—like career changes, family obligations, or health issues—can also strain emotional connections. Recognizing these stressors and addressing them as a team can help preserve the integrity of the relationship.

Consider the story of Lily and Sam, a couple who faced the test of time with grace and commitment. Married for over two decades, they prioritised communication and quality time above all else. Every Saturday, without fail, they would have breakfast together, phones off, just the two of them. This ritual became their anchor, a way to check in and stay connected amid life's chaos. They also embraced the art of conversation, never shying away from difficult topics but approaching them with curiosity and respect. By doing so, they not only strengthened their bond but also modelled a relationship grounded in mutual respect and understanding.

Successful long-term relationships often share a common thread: the willingness to adapt and evolve together. Couples who thrive are those who embrace change as an opportunity for growth, rather than a threat to stability. They're open to trying new things, exploring new activities, and even revisiting old ones with fresh perspectives. This adaptability keeps the relationship dynamic, ensuring it doesn't fall into the trap of monotony. It's about finding joy in the little things, celebrating each other's successes, and offering comfort during setbacks. These shared experiences create a tapestry of connection that weaves through the fabric of time.

Maintaining emotional bonds over the years isn't always easy, but it's undoubtedly rewarding. It requires effort, patience, and a commitment to nurturing the relationship continuously. By investing in these connections, you cultivate a partnership that is resilient, fulfilling, and deeply rooted in love. As you turn the page to the next chapter, consider how these practices can enrich your own relationships, creating a foundation that withstands the test of time.

4

Chapter 4: Self-Discovery and Personal Growth

Once, during a particularly challenging week, I found myself at a quiet park, sitting on a bench with a notebook in hand. I had no specific agenda, just a desire to untangle the emotional knots I felt tightening inside. As I scribbled down thoughts and feelings, I noticed a shift—a clarity emerging from the pages. It was as if each word lifted a weight off my shoulders, leaving me lighter and more in tune with myself. This was self-reflection at work, a powerful tool that helps you understand your emotional needs and navigate the complexities of life with greater awareness.

Self-reflection is like holding a mirror up to your soul, allowing you to see the intricate dance of thoughts, emotions, and behaviours that define your inner world. It's a process of introspection that goes beyond the surface, helping you gain deeper insights into your motivations and patterns (Source 1). Imagine keeping a daily journal, where you jot down your experiences and emotions. This simple act can be incredibly revealing. It's not about writing a novel; it's about capturing those fleeting thoughts and feelings that often get lost in the hustle and bustle of daily life. Over time, these entries become a map of your emotional landscape, showing you where you've been and guiding you towards where you want to go.

Meditation is another powerful practice for introspection. It's like taking a mental pause, a chance to tune out the noise and tune into yourself. By focusing on your breath or a mantra, you allow your mind to settle, creating space for clarity and insight. It's not about emptying your mind completely—let's be real, who can do that?—but about observing your thoughts without judgement. This practice can help you identify emotional triggers, those sneaky little things that set off a cascade of feelings. Reflecting on past experiences that elicited strong emotions can also be enlightening. Maybe it was a heated argument with a friend or a moment of pure joy. By examining these instances, you can pinpoint what stirs your emotions and why, equipping you with the knowledge to navigate future situations with greater ease.

To facilitate self-reflection, consider using guided self-assessment questionnaires. These tools can help you dig deeper, asking questions that prompt introspection and self-discovery. They're like a personal trainer for your mind, pushing you to explore areas you might otherwise overlook. Seeking feedback from trusted friends or mentors can also provide valuable perspectives. Sometimes, an outside view can highlight patterns you might not see on your own, offering insights that enrich your understanding of yourself.

Understanding your emotional needs brings numerous benefits. It's like finding the right key to unlock better communication and satisfaction in your relationships. When you're clear about what you need emotionally, you can express it to others more effectively. This clarity leads to improved conflict resolution skills, as you're better equipped to articulate your feelings and understand those of others. Imagine a scenario where you feel upset with a partner but can't quite put your finger on why. Through self-reflection, you discover that it's not about the dirty dishes left in the sink, but about feeling unappreciated. Armed with this insight, you can communicate your needs more clearly, paving the way for a resolution that addresses the root of the issue rather than just the symptoms.

Interactive Element: Emotional Needs Checklist

Consider creating an Emotional Needs Checklist to help you identify and articulate what you need to feel emotionally fulfilled. List out various needs like trust, appreciation, independence, or support. Rank them by importance and note any that are unmet. Use this checklist as a conversation starter with those you trust, helping them understand how to support you better. This exercise can clarify your emotional landscape and empower you to take proactive steps towards fulfillment.

Finding Your Inner Strength: A Personal Journey

Inner strength is like a quiet force within you, ready to rise when the going gets tough. It's not about being unbreakable, but about having the resilience to bounce back from life's challenges. It's that inner voice that says, "You've got this," even when the world feels overwhelming. Inner strength isn't something you're born with; it's cultivated through experiences, both good and bad. It's about learning from setbacks, picking yourself up, and moving forward with newfound wisdom. This strength allows you to overcome obstacles, face fears, and navigate the complexities of life with confidence and grace.

Consider the story of Maya, a young woman who found herself at a crossroads after losing her job. At first, the uncertainty was daunting, and self-doubt crept in. But instead of giving up, she chose to view this setback as an opportunity for growth. Maya enrolled in a course that aligned with her passion, and through dedication and perseverance, she discovered a new career path that fulfilled her. Her journey wasn't easy, filled with moments of doubt and frustration, but her resilience and determination were her guiding lights. Maya's story is a testament to the power of personal growth and the strength that emerges from embracing change. It's through these experiences that you, too, can uncover your inner strength and resilience.

Building inner strength is an ongoing process, like training a muscle. Start by setting personal goals that challenge and inspire you. They don't have to be monumental; even small, attainable goals can create momentum. Achieving these goals boosts your confidence and reinforces your belief in your capabilities. Developing a positive mindset is equally crucial. Affirmations can be a powerful tool—simple statements like "I am capable" or "I trust myself" can shift your perspective and empower you to face challenges head-on. It's about nurturing a mindset that focuses on growth and possibility rather than fear and limitation. Surrounding yourself with supportive individuals who uplift and encourage you can also make a significant difference.

In relationships, inner strength plays a vital role. It allows you to support your partner while maintaining your own identity. You can be there for them, offering empathy and understanding, without losing sight of your own needs and desires. This balance is crucial for healthy relationships, as it fosters mutual respect and growth. Imagine being in a relationship where both partners encourage each other's dreams, celebrating successes and offering support during setbacks. This dynamic creates a partnership where both individuals feel valued and empowered to pursue their aspirations. Inner strength also helps you set healthy boundaries, ensuring that your needs are met without compromising your values.

Take, for instance, the relationship of Emma and Alex. Emma has always been passionate about art, while Alex thrives in the world of finance. Instead of viewing these differences as a divide, they saw them as opportunities for learning and growth. Emma often attended Alex's work events, supporting him with genuine interest, while Alex made time to appreciate Emma's art shows. Their relationship thrived because they respected each other's individuality and encouraged personal growth. Emma's inner strength allowed her to pursue her passion without losing herself in the relationship, while Alex's resilience helped him adapt and grow alongside her. This balance of support and independence is a hallmark of strong, healthy relationships, where both parties can flourish without fear of overshadowing or being overshadowed.

Empowerment Through Self-Love

Self-love is a powerful force that can change your life in more ways than one. It's not just about pampering yourself with spa days or treating yourself to your favourite meals—though those are lovely, too. At its core, self-love is about recognizing your worth and treating yourself with the same kindness and respect you show others. Think of it as the foundation upon which you build your sense of self. When you truly love yourself, you empower your well-being and transform your relationships. You become more in tune with who you are and what you need. Self-love allows you to stand tall in the face of challenges, knowing you're enough just as you are.

Embracing self-love often requires a shift in mindset. Picture someone who once measured their value by their achievements or how they were perceived by others. They constantly strive for perfection, never feeling quite "good enough." But one day, they decided to practise self-compassion, allowing themselves to be human, to make mistakes, and to learn from them. They let go of the need to be perfect, realising that perfection is an illusion. This acceptance opened the door to self-love, giving them the freedom to celebrate their uniqueness and embrace their flaws. Practising self-compassion in daily life means forgiving yourself when things don't go as planned. It's giving yourself a break when you're tired or overwhelmed and speaking to yourself with kindness rather than criticism.

Cultivating self-love involves taking active steps to nurture your relationship with yourself. One simple exercise is creating a self-appreciation list. Take some time to jot down qualities you admire in yourself, achievements you're proud of, and moments when you've shown strength or kindness. Keep this list handy, so you can refer to it whenever you're feeling down or doubting yourself. Another powerful practice is engaging in daily self-affirmations. Each morning, look in the mirror and speak words of encouragement. Say things like, "I am worthy of love and respect," or "I am capable of achieving my dreams." It might feel a bit awkward at first, but over time, these affirmations can reshape your inner dialogue, building a foundation of self-love and confidence.

This newfound self-love doesn't just benefit you; it also

empowers your relationships. When you love yourself, you no longer seek validation from others to feel complete. You establish healthy boundaries, understanding that it's okay to say no when something doesn't serve your well-being. This self-respect fosters mutual respect in relationships, enhancing communication and understanding. Imagine being in a relationship where both partners are secure in themselves and respect each other's needs and boundaries. There's no need for jealousy or insecurity, as both individuals bring their whole selves to the table. This creates a dynamic where love and respect flow freely, enriching the relationship.

In relationships, self-love enables you to engage with others from a place of abundance rather than lack. You're less likely to cling to others for security because you've found that security within. This inner peace enhances your ability to support your partner without losing sight of your own identity. You're able to celebrate each other's successes, comfort each other during setbacks, and grow together in harmony. Self-love acts as a catalyst for deeper connections, where both partners feel valued and understood. It sets the stage for a relationship where love is not about filling a void but about sharing life's journey with someone who complements your wholeness.

The beauty of self-love lies in its ability to transform not only how you see yourself but also how you relate to the world around you. It's a lifelong practice that evolves as you do, continually enriching your life and relationships. As you nurture this self-love, you'll find that it empowers you to live authentically, embrace your true self, and engage with others in ways that are meaningful and fulfilling.

Overcoming Insecurities in Love

Insecurities in relationships often creep in like shadows, casting doubt and fear. One of the most common insecurities is the fear of abandonment. It's that unsettling feeling that arises when you start to question whether your partner might leave you. This fear can stem from past experiences, like a previous relationship where trust was broken, or even from witnessing similar situations in others' lives. Doubts about self-worth often accompany this fear. You might catch yourself thinking, "Am I really good enough?" or "What if they find someone better?" These thoughts can become a relentless cycle, feeding off each other until they feel overwhelming.

To address these insecurities, you can employ strategies that challenge these negative thoughts. Cognitive-behavioural techniques are a powerful tool. They help you identify and reframe those nagging doubts, turning "I'm not good enough" into "I am worthy of love and respect." Start by writing down your negative thoughts, then challenge them. Ask yourself, "Is this thought based on facts or just fears?" This process helps you see your insecurities for what they are—unfounded fears rather than truths. Building trust through open communication with your partner is equally important. Share your feelings and concerns honestly, allowing your partner to understand and support you. When you express vulnerability, it invites your partner to do the same, creating a space where trust can flourish.

Unchecked insecurities can wreak havoc on relationships. They can lead to unnecessary conflicts, where misunderstandings and assumptions replace healthy communication. Imagine accusing your partner of being distant because you fear losing them, only to realise later that they were simply preoccupied with work. These conflicts often arise from a place of fear rather than reality, damaging the relationship's foundation. Insecurities can also lead to defensive behaviours, like withdrawing emotionally or becoming overly clingy. Both responses create distance rather than closeness, preventing the relationship from growing and thriving.

To combat these challenges, it's crucial to build confidence and reduce insecurity. Mindfulness meditation is a practice that can increase self-awareness and bring a sense of calm. By focusing on the present moment, you learn to observe your thoughts without judgement, reducing their power over you. This increased awareness helps you recognize insecurity-driven behaviours before they escalate. Additionally, engaging in activities that boost self-confidence, like pursuing hobbies or setting achievable goals, can reinforce a positive self-image. Celebrate your accomplishments, no matter how small, and remind yourself of your strengths and capabilities.

When you work on overcoming these insecurities, you create a more balanced and fulfilling relationship. You'll find that as your confidence grows, your need for constant reassurance diminishes. This newfound security allows you to engage with your partner from a place of love rather than fear. You become more attuned to each other's needs, fostering a deeper connection and understanding. Insecurities might not disappear entirely, but you learn to manage them, preventing them from overshadowing the joy and love you share. As you navigate these challenges, you'll discover that true connection thrives not in the absence of insecurity but in the presence of trust and mutual support.

Personal Growth as a Foundation for Healthy Relationships

Personal growth and relationships are like two strands of DNA, intricately woven together, each influencing the other in profound ways. When you focus on personal development, you not only enhance your own life but also elevate the quality of your relationships. This growth provides a solid foundation, allowing you to engage with others from a place of strength and self-awareness. As you evolve, your relationships can thrive, becoming more resilient and fulfilling. Picture a couple who encourages each other's aspirations, celebrating every step along their individual paths. They understand that their personal achievements contribute to a shared success, enriching their bond. This dynamic fosters a sense of partnership where both individuals feel supported and valued. Embracing change as a couple is another hallmark of thriving relationships. Change is inevitable, and those who welcome it with open arms often find new opportunities for connection and growth. Imagine facing life's twists and turns together, adapting and learning from each experience. This adaptability strengthens your bond, creating a relationship that is both dynamic and enduring.

To actively pursue personal growth, consider enrolling in skill-building workshops. These can range from cooking classes to coding bootcamps, offering new perspectives and skills that enrich your life. Engaging in continuous learning not only enhances your self-esteem but also brings fresh energy into your relationships. Setting personal and relational goals is another powerful strategy. By identifying what you want to achieve individually and as a couple, you create a roadmap for growth. This shared vision fosters collaboration and mutual support, ensuring that both partners feel invested in each other's success. It's like planting a garden, where each goal is a seed that, with care and attention, blossoms into a vibrant display of growth and fulfillment.

Adopting a growth mindset in relationships encourages both individuals to view challenges as opportunities for development. This mindset emphasises progress over perfection, allowing you to celebrate small victories and learn from setbacks. Imagine approaching a disagreement not as a failure, but as a chance to understand each other better. This perspective fosters empathy and communication, strengthening your connection. When you focus on progress, you create an environment where both partners feel empowered to grow and evolve. This mindset also encourages vulnerability, as you both learn to embrace imperfections and support each other through the ups and downs.

Consider the story of Jake and Zoe, who both decided to pursue their passions—Jake in photography and Zoe in environmental science. Instead of seeing these pursuits as separate endeavours, they embraced them as opportunities to grow together. Jake often accompanied Zoe on field trips, capturing the beauty of nature through his lens, while Zoe used her scientific knowledge to teach Jake about the ecosystems they explored. Their shared experiences deepened their bond, fostering a relationship where personal growth and connection thrived hand in hand. This balance of individuality and partnership allowed them to support each other's dreams while maintaining a strong, unified relationship.

Personal growth is the foundation upon which healthy relationships are built. As you continue to invest in your development, you'll find that your relationships are enriched by the insights and skills you gain. This chapter has explored how personal growth supports and enhances relationships, offering strategies to actively pursue development. Remember, growth is a journey, not a destination, and each step forward brings new opportunities for connection and fulfillment. With a focus on progress and a willingness to embrace change, you'll create relationships that are dynamic, resilient, and deeply rewarding.

As we move forward, we'll explore how these principles apply to the digital age, where technology and connection intersect in new and exciting ways.

5

Chapter 5: Love in the Digital Age

Imagine this: you're scrolling through your favourite social media platform, and suddenly you spot a post that makes your heart skip a beat. It's not the latest fashion trend or a meme that's gone viral—though those are fun too—but a photo of your friend's relationship milestone. Maybe it's their first anniversary or a cute post marking their relationship as "Facebook official." You smile and hit the like button, feeling a surge of joy for them. Yet, beneath that initial happiness, a tiny voice whispers, "Why isn't my relationship like that?" This is the digital age, where love and relationships unfold not just in private moments but also on the public stage of social media.

Social media has undeniably transformed how we communicate and connect. Platforms like Instagram and Snapchat have become integral parts of our daily lives, allowing us to stay in touch with loved ones across distances. They provide a window into each other's worlds, fostering a sense of togetherness. In relationships, social media can serve as a platform for expressing affection and celebrating milestones. A simple post declaring your love can feel like shouting from the rooftops, reaching

47

friends and family far and wide. However, this digital display is a double-edged sword. While it can strengthen bonds, it can also introduce challenges that previous generations never faced.

One of the most significant challenges in digital relationships is the jealousy sparked by online interactions. Ever notice a pang of insecurity when your partner likes or comments on someone else's post? You're not alone. According to a survey by Pew Research Center, 23% of partnered adults feel jealous or unsure about their relationship due to their partner's social media interactions (Source 1). This jealousy often stems from misinterpretations, as online cues lack the nuances of face-to-face communication. A comment intended as a friendly gesture might be perceived as flirtatious, leading to misunderstandings and unnecessary tension.

To navigate these digital waters, setting boundaries for social media use is crucial. It's like having a roadmap that guides you through potential pitfalls, ensuring you don't veer off course. Start by discussing with your partner what feels comfortable for both of you. Agree on what's acceptable in terms of online interactions and what crosses the line. This proactive approach can prevent minor issues from escalating into major conflicts. Open communication is also key. Share your feelings about social media interactions, and listen to your partner's perspective. By fostering an environment where both parties feel heard, you can address concerns before they become problems.

As you engage with social media, remember the importance of privacy. In a world where oversharing is common, it's tempting to post every detail of your life online. But maintaining some level of privacy is vital for a healthy relationship. Avoid sharing personal details that might compromise your privacy or your partner's. This includes everything from intimate conversations to private disagreements. Public digital displays of affection can be sweet, but they should never replace personal, heartfelt moments shared in private. Understanding the impact of these displays helps maintain a balance between public and private aspects of your relationship.

Interactive Element: Social Media Boundaries Checklist

Consider creating a Social Media Boundaries Checklist with your partner. Include points such as acceptable interactions, how often you'll post about your relationship, and what topics are off-limits for public sharing. Revisit this checklist periodically to ensure it still aligns with both of your comfort levels. This exercise can serve as a guide, helping you navigate the digital landscape with confidence and mutual respect.

In this digital age, love and relationships are evolving in fascinating ways. Social media offers opportunities to connect and communicate like never before, but it also presents unique challenges. By setting clear boundaries, communicating openly, and valuing privacy, you can harness the positive aspects of digital engagement while safeguarding your relationship from potential pitfalls. The key is to remain mindful of how you interact online and to prioritise genuine connections over curated digital personas. In doing so, you'll find that love in the digital age can be as fulfilling and rewarding as ever, enriched by the tools and platforms that connect us all.

Digital Intimacy: Building Connections Online

Digital intimacy might sound like a contradiction at first, but it's a fascinating concept that's become increasingly relevant in our tech-savvy world. Unlike traditional forms of intimacy, where face-to-face interaction is key, digital intimacy is about forging emotional connections through online platforms. Imagine two people, continents apart, feeling close despite the miles. It's the magic of technology, allowing hearts to connect through screens. Platforms like video calls create spaces where you can see and hear each other, bridging the gap in ways letters or emails never could. These calls bring faces to life, allowing you to share a smile or a meaningful look, even if you're oceans away.

Messaging apps have also revolutionised how we maintain connections. With just a few taps, you can share your day, your thoughts, or even a silly meme that made you laugh. This constant communication keeps the conversation flowing, ensuring that you remain a part of each other's daily lives. Whether you're sharing good morning texts or arguing over who would win in a superhero face-off, these interactions weave a tapestry of shared experiences. It's like having a digital thread that ties you together, no matter where life takes you. While traditional intimacy often relies on proximity, digital intimacy thrives on accessibility, offering a unique way to maintain closeness in a fast-paced world.

The benefits of digital intimacy are especially apparent in long-distance relationships. For couples separated by geography, digital tools become lifelines. They offer a way to bridge the physical divide, making it possible to share moments that might otherwise be missed. You can watch a movie together, syncing your screens while chatting about plot twists or favourite scenes. It's a shared experience, bringing a sense of normalcy to the distance. These digital dates, whether it's a virtual dinner or a game night, create opportunities to connect, laugh, and grow closer. The technology becomes an ally, helping you nurture the relationship despite the miles.

However, digital intimacy isn't without its challenges. One significant pitfall is the potential for miscommunication. Without physical presence, it's easy to misinterpret messages or miss the subtle nuances of tone and body language. A text meant to be lighthearted might come across as blunt, sparking confusion or conflict. This lack of nonverbal cues can lead to misunderstandings that wouldn't occur in person. Additionally, there's the risk of emotional disconnect due to over-reliance on technology. It's tempting to substitute digital interactions for genuine connection, but screens can only do so much. The absence of physical touch and presence can create a sense of longing that technology can't fully satisfy.

To navigate these challenges, it's crucial to balance digital interactions with authentic engagement. Make an effort to express emotions clearly, using emojis or clarifying phrases to convey your intent. When miscommunication arises, address it openly, ensuring that both parties feel understood. It's about creating a safe space where concerns can be voiced and resolved. Alongside digital communication, prioritise physical meetings whenever possible, even if they're infrequent. These moments of real-world connection can reinforce the digital bond, grounding the relationship in shared experiences and memories.

Apps designed for couples can also play a role in enhancing digital intimacy. From games that spark conversation to tools that help manage shared tasks, these apps provide creative ways to connect. They encourage interaction beyond the typical text or call, offering new avenues for engagement. Whether it's a quiz that helps you learn more about each other or a planner that ensures you never miss an important date, these tools can enrich your digital connection. They add variety to your interactions, keeping things fresh and exciting.

Digital intimacy is an evolving concept, reflecting the ways technology reshapes our relationships. It offers a means to connect, communicate, and grow closer, even when distance is a factor. While it presents unique challenges, with thoughtful engagement and a focus on genuine connection, digital intimacy can enhance relationships, bringing people together in meaningful ways.

Avoiding Comparisons in a Curated World

Scrolling through social media can sometimes feel like flipping through a glossy magazine. Everything seems perfect—every photo is filtered to perfection, every moment captured is a highlight. It's like everyone is living in a constant state of bliss, and it's easy to start believing that. Social media encourages us to present idealised versions of our lives, using filters and editing tools that smooth out imperfections and amplify the good. It creates a highlight reel, a polished version of reality where only the best moments make the cut. This curated content can be inspiring, sure, but it can also set unrealistic expectations that leave you feeling inadequate. You see your friends posting about romantic getaways, perfect date nights, and seemingly flawless relationships, and you wonder why your life doesn't measure up.

The impact of these comparisons can seep into your relationships, creating an undercurrent of envy and dissatisfaction. It's like looking through a window at a world where everything is shinier and more exciting, making your own reality seem dull in comparison. This kind of relationship envy can lead to unnecessary tension and doubts. You might start questioning your own experiences, wondering if they're as meaningful or exciting as what others are sharing online. But remember, social media is a curated space. People tend to share their successes, glossing over the struggles and mundane moments that make up the rest of their lives. It's like a movie trailer—highlighting the best parts while leaving out the messy, complicated scenes.

To resist the urge to compare, practising gratitude can be a powerful antidote. Focus on your personal achievements and the unique aspects of your relationship that bring you joy. It's about shifting your perspective from what you don't have to what you do. Consider keeping a gratitude journal where you jot down moments that make you smile, whether it's a shared laugh with your partner or a small victory in your personal life. This practice can help ground you in reality, reminding you that your life and relationships are valuable and meaningful, even if they don't always look Instagram-perfect.

Another effective strategy is limiting your exposure to social media during vulnerable times. If you're feeling down or insecure, stepping away from the curated world of social media can offer a much-needed break. It's like giving yourself permission to breathe, without the distraction of polished posts and filtered realities. Use this time to reconnect with yourself and your loved ones in more meaningful ways. Engage in activities that nurture your well-being, whether it's spending time in nature, diving into a hobby, or enjoying a heartfelt conversation with a friend.

These real-world experiences can offer a richer, more fulfilling sense of connection than any number of likes or comments.

Self-awareness is a crucial tool in navigating the digital landscape. By understanding your own relationship dynamics, you can better appreciate the unique qualities that make your connections special. Journaling about your personal feelings and thoughts can be a great way to cultivate this awareness. Take time to reflect on what makes your relationships meaningful, noting the qualities and moments that you value. This self-reflection can help you stay grounded, providing clarity about what truly matters to you. Engaging in activities that promote self-awareness, like meditation or mindfulness exercises, can also support this process. They encourage you to tune into your inner world, fostering a deeper understanding of your needs and desires.

In a world where social media sets a high bar for perfection, it's important to remember that real life is beautifully imperfect. Your relationship might not always look like a fairytale, but that doesn't diminish its worth. Embrace the quirks, the challenges, and the joys that make your connections uniquely yours. By focusing on authenticity and staying true to yourself, you can navigate the curated world of social media with confidence and grace, celebrating your own path without the need for comparison.

Authentic Communication in a Digital Landscape

In today's digital world, authentic communication is like the golden ticket—a way to genuinely connect amidst a sea of digital noise. But what does it mean to communicate authentically online? It's about being genuine in your interactions, showing your true self despite the carefully curated digital personas that many people present. Authenticity means your online presence mirrors your real-life self, without the filters or masks that can sometimes come with social media. It's expressing your thoughts and feelings honestly, whether you're sending a text, posting a comment, or sharing a photo. When you stay true to who you are, your online interactions become more meaningful, allowing for real connections that go beyond the superficial.

Yet, maintaining this authenticity online isn't always easy. One major barrier is the presence of digital personas and avatars. These avatars can create a disconnect between who we are and how we present ourselves online. It's like having a digital mask that only shows the parts of ourselves we want others to see. This can lead to interactions that feel hollow or insincere. There's also the pressure to conform to online trends, to post the perfect selfie or share the most relatable meme. The fear of missing out can push us to engage in ways that don't feel true to our personalities. Navigating these pressures requires conscious effort and a willingness to push back against the tide of conformity.

So how can you ensure your online communications remain genuine and true? Start by using voice notes to convey tone and emotion. Sometimes, words on a screen can feel flat or lack the warmth you intend. A voice note adds a personal touch, allowing your personality to shine through. It's like adding colour to a black-and-white sketch. Personalising your messages beyond generic responses is another effective strategy. Instead of a simple "LOL" or "Congrats," take a moment to share a specific memory or compliment. This not only enriches the conversation but also shows the recipient that you care. It's these little touches that make interactions feel special and authentic.

The benefits of maintaining authenticity online are significant. For starters, it builds trust through honest interactions. When you consistently present your true self, people know they can rely on your words. This trust is invaluable in digital relation-ships, where misunderstandings can easily occur. Authenticity also strengthens bonds by sharing real-life experiences. When you're open about your joys and struggles, you invite others to do the same, creating a space for mutual support and under-standing. It's like planting seeds in a garden; with time and care, these interactions blossom into strong, lasting connections.

To illustrate, consider a digital friendship that began with a shared interest. Over time, this friendship grew as both individuals shared more about their personal lives—triumphs, challenges, and everything in between. By being transparent and genuine, they developed a bond that felt as meaningful as any face-to-face friendship. This is the power of authentic communication online. It transcends the digital divide, allowing you to connect with others on a deep and personal level.

As we navigate the complexities of digital communication, re-member that authenticity is your anchor. It keeps you grounded, reminding you of who you are and what you value. In a world where digital personas can often feel like facades, your true self is your greatest asset. Embrace it, and let it guide you in building connections that are both rich and rewarding.

6

Chapter 6: Overcoming Relationship Challenges

Imagine standing in front of a mirror, scrutinising every flaw and imperfection. You might find yourself thinking, "Why can't I just be enough?" This moment of self-doubt is all too familiar for many of us. It creeps into our relationships, whispering that we need to do more, be more, or have more to be loved. This chapter is about addressing those insecurities, not by looking outward for material reassurance, but by cultivating a deeper understanding and acceptance of ourselves. Let's explore how we can transform these doubts into opportunities for growth and connection.

Addressing Insecurity Without Material Reassurance

Understanding the roots of insecurity is a bit like unravelling a tangled ball of yarn. It often stems from our childhood experiences, where the seeds of self-perception are first planted. According to Attachment Theory, early relationships with caregivers play a significant role in shaping our sense of security. If those bonds were inconsistent or absent, we might carry doubts about our self-worth into adulthood, fearing rejection or abandonment in our relationships. Past betrayals can also leave scars, creating a protective shell of distrust. These experiences contribute to a complex emotional state where insecurity thrives, influencing how we interact with loved ones and perceive ourselves.

To combat these insecurities, developing self-compassion is key. It's about treating yourself with the same kindness and understanding you'd offer a friend. Start with daily affirmations of self-worth. Each morning, look in the mirror and tell yourself something positive. "I am deserving of love and respect" or "I am enough just as I am" are powerful reminders that can shift your mindset. Mindfulness meditation is another tool to help you focus on self-acceptance. By sitting quietly and observing your thoughts without judgement, you create space for acceptance and healing. This practice helps you become more aware of your self-critical tendencies, allowing you to replace them with compassion and empathy.

Fostering open communication with your partner is crucial in addressing insecurities. It's about creating a safe space where you can share your fears and vulnerabilities without fear of judgement. Regular check-ins about your emotional well-being can strengthen your bond and build trust. These conversations don't have to be formal sit-downs; they can happen during a walk or while cooking dinner together. The key is to be honest and open, expressing your feelings and listening to your partner's in return. By doing so, you cultivate an environment where both of you feel valued and understood, reducing the reliance on material reassurances to feel secure.

Cultivating internal validation requires a shift from seeking approval outside to finding it within. Journaling can be a transformative practice in this journey. Take time to reflect on your achievements and personal growth. Celebrate your successes, no matter how small, and acknowledge the progress you've made. This exercise reinforces your self-worth and highlights your capabilities, helping you see yourself in a more positive light. Engaging in hobbies that boost your self-esteem is another way to nurture internal validation. Whether it's painting, writing, or dancing, find something that brings you joy and allows you to express yourself authentically. These activities provide a sense of accomplishment and fulfillment, reminding you that you are enough without needing external validation.

Reflection Prompt: The Self-Compassion Journal

Consider starting a self-compassion journal. Each evening, write down three things you appreciate about yourself. They can be qualities, achievements, or even simple acts of kindness you showed that day. Over time, this practice can help you build a foundation of self-love and acceptance, reducing the need for material reassurance. It's a small step, but one that can lead to profound changes in how you perceive yourself and your relationships.

As you embark on this journey of self-discovery and growth, remember that overcoming insecurities is not about erasing them entirely. It's about recognizing them, understanding their origins, and transforming them into opportunities for connection and empowerment. By addressing these challenges, you open the door to deeper, more fulfilling relationships, where love is not measured by material possessions but by genuine connection and mutual respect.

Navigating Peer Pressure in Relationships

Imagine this: you're out with friends, and the topic of relation-ships comes up. Everyone seems to have an opinion about who you should be dating or how you should act in your relationship. Their voices become a chorus, echoing societal norms and expectations. This is where peer pressure begins to weave its subtle web, influencing your thoughts and actions more than you might realise. Friends can have a significant impact on your relationship dynamics, sometimes without you even noticing. They might suggest that you need to find someone who fits a certain mould or that you should expect grand gestures of love to prove your partner's commitment. It's like an invisible hand guiding you, often steering you away from your true desires and values.

Societal expectations also play a huge role, telling us what love should look like. The pressure to conform can feel over-whelming. Maybe you've felt this when scrolling through social media, where perfectly curated relationships seem to set an unattainable standard. It's all too easy to let these external influences dictate your choices, leading to decisions that don't align with your authentic self. Recognizing these pressures is crucial, as it allows you to start untangling yourself from their grip. It's about stepping back and asking, "Is this what I truly want, or is this what I've been told I should want?"

To combat these pressures, building assertiveness is key. Think of it as strengthening a muscle—one that allows you to stand firm in your beliefs and choices despite the noise around you. Role-playing scenarios can be an effective way to practise this skill. Imagine a situation where a friend questions your relationship choices. How would you respond? Practising these conversations in a safe environment can prepare you for real-life situations, boosting your confidence. Setting clear personal boundaries with peers is equally important. It's about respectfully communicating your limits and making it known that while you value their opinions, your decisions are ultimately your own. This boundary-setting not only protects your relationship but also strengthens it, as you learn to prioritise what truly matters to you.

Encouraging independent decision-making is another crucial step. It's about empowering yourself to make choices based on your personal values, not on what others think is best. Start by reflecting on your relationship goals. What do you want in a partner? What are your deal-breakers? By clearly defining these aspects, you create a roadmap that guides your decisions. This reflection allows you to align your choices with your own desires, rather than being swayed by external pressures. It's like having a compass that always points to your true north, ensuring you stay on a path that feels right for you.

Resisting peer pressure can lead to more fulfilling and authentic relationships. When you make decisions based on your values, you experience increased relationship satisfaction. You're not constantly second-guessing yourself or wondering if you're living up to someone else's expectations. Instead, you find joy in being true to yourself and your partner. This authenticity creates a deeper connection, where both individuals feel seen and valued for who they truly are. Greater alignment with personal values not only enhances your relationship but also boosts your self-esteem, as you learn to trust in your own judgement and capabilities.

The benefits of staying true to oneself extend beyond the relationship itself. They ripple into every aspect of your life, fostering a sense of autonomy and empowerment. You become more attuned to your own needs and desires, cultivating a life that reflects your genuine self. This authenticity attracts like-minded individuals who appreciate you for who you are, further enriching your social circle. As you continue to navigate the complexities of relationships and peer pressure, remember that your choices are yours to make. Embrace the freedom that comes with living authentically, and let it guide you toward relationships that resonate with your true self.

Establishing Boundaries in a Material World

In a world that often measures worth by what you own or can give, setting boundaries becomes more than just a personal preference—it's an act of self-preservation. Boundaries serve as invisible shields that protect your emotional and mental well-being, acting like a fence that keeps outside pressures from trampling your inner peace. Imagine walking through a field, free to enjoy the flowers without worrying about someone suddenly turning your path into a tug-of-war over possessions. Boundaries create that kind of freedom in relationships, ensuring that you aren't swept away by expectations that don't serve your true self. They are the lines you draw to maintain your identity and sanity.

In today's materialistic society, boundaries also play a crucial role in preventing financial exploitation. Picture a scenario where a friend continually suggests splitting costs for extravagant things you can't afford. Without clear boundaries, you might find yourself in a financial bind, stressing over money rather than enjoying the time spent together. By establishing boundaries, you communicate your financial limits, allowing you to enjoy relationships without the weight of financial strain. It's like setting a budget for your emotions and wallet, ensuring you don't overspend in either area.

Setting effective boundaries requires clear communication and consistency. Imagine you're at a party, and someone offers you a drink you don't want. Saying "no" confidently and assertively, without wavering, is like planting a flag in the ground, signalling that your boundaries are firm. This approach applies to emotional and material boundaries alike. When you communicate your limits clearly, whether it's declining an extravagant gift that makes you uncomfortable or opting out of material competitions, you set the tone for how others should engage with you. Consistency is key here. If you waver or give in, it sends a mixed message, inviting future boundary challenges.

Consider a real-life scenario where a friend insists on buying you expensive gifts, even when you've expressed discomfort. Saying no can feel awkward, like turning down a second slice of cake at a party, but it's necessary to maintain your comfort and integrity. You might say, "I appreciate your generosity, but I prefer to keep things simple." This statement honours your boundary while acknowledging their intention. In another instance, you might find yourself in a group where everyone is caught up in a cycle of one-upmanship, competing over who has the latest gadget. Declining to participate in these competitions can feel like stepping out of a whirlwind, allowing you to catch your breath and stay true to your values.

Boundaries can be challenged, especially when others are used to crossing them. It's like adjusting to a new pair of shoes; there might be some initial resistance, but once you settle in, they provide the support and comfort you need. Reaffirming your boundaries with empathy is crucial. If someone repeatedly tests your limits, calmly restate your position. You might say, "I understand you enjoy these outings, but I need to stick to my spending limits." This reinforces your stance while showing understanding. If the challenge persists, seeking support from trusted friends or professionals can provide guidance and strength. Sometimes, an outside perspective can offer strategies to uphold your boundaries without straining your relationships.

Boundaries aren't just protective barriers; they're bridges to healthier connections. By maintaining them, you build relationships based on mutual respect and understanding. They allow you to engage with others from a place of authenticity, where your values and comfort are prioritised over external pressures. In a world that often equates love with material gestures, boundaries remind you that true connection isn't about what you give or receive but about who you are and how you relate to others.

Resolving Conflicts with Emotional Intelligence

Picture this: you're in the middle of a heated argument with your partner, words flying faster than you can catch them. It feels like you're both speaking different languages, and no one's really listening. This is where emotional intelligence, or EI, comes into play. At its core, emotional intelligence is about being aware of and managing your emotions while understanding and empathising with others. It's like having a toolbox for your feelings, offering tools to navigate conflicts smoothly. Self-awareness is a key component here—it's about recognizing your emotional responses and understanding why you react the way you do. When you know what's going on inside, you can handle your emotions better, preventing them from taking control of the situation.

Empathy is another crucial aspect. It's the ability to step into your partner's shoes and see things from their perspective. It's like being a detective, piecing together clues about how they're feeling and why. This understanding can transform a confrontation into a conversation. By practising empathy, you create a bridge of understanding that allows you to connect on a deeper level, even when emotions are running high. Empathy doesn't mean agreeing with everything your partner says, but it does mean respecting their feelings and striving to understand their point of view.

When it comes to practical strategies for resolving disputes, active listening is your best friend. Imagine listening to someone not just to respond but to truly understand their perspective. It's about being fully present, giving them your undivided attention, and acknowledging their feelings. This simple act can defuse tension and pave the way for productive dialogue. Using "I" statements is another powerful technique. Instead of saying, "You never listen to me," try, "I feel unheard when we talk about this." This approach focuses on your feelings rather than placing blame, which can prevent defensiveness and open the door to resolution.

Perspective-taking is an art, but it's one worth mastering. It involves seeing the world through your partner's eyes, understanding their motivations and concerns. Imagine a painter stepping back from their canvas to see the full picture, rather than getting lost in the details. This practice allows you to approach conflicts with an open mind, looking for solutions that benefit both parties. Empathy exercises can help you develop this skill. Try imagining how you would feel in your partner's situation, or even switch roles in a hypothetical scenario to gain insight into their experience. By doing so, you cultivate a mindset that prioritises understanding over winning an argument.

Let's delve into a story of a couple who effectively used emotional intelligence to resolve their conflicts. Meet Sarah and Jake. They often found themselves bickering over small things, like whose turn it was to do the dishes or plan a date night. One day, they decided to try something different. During their next disagreement, they agreed to pause and listen to each other without interrupting. Sarah shared her feelings using "I" statements, explaining that she felt overwhelmed with work and needed more support at home. Jake listened, empathised, and acknowledged her feelings. He then expressed his own concerns about feeling unappreciated. This calm communication de-escalated the argument, allowing them to find a win-win solution: a schedule that balanced their responsibilities and acknowledged each other's needs.

This example highlights the power of emotional intelligence in resolving conflicts. By approaching disagreements with empathy, self-awareness, and effective communication, you can transform potential arguments into opportunities for growth and connection. It's about shifting from a combative mindset to one that seeks understanding and collaboration. With these tools, conflicts become less about winning and more about building stronger, more resilient relationships.

As we wrap up this chapter on overcoming relationship challenges, remember that these strategies are not about eliminating conflicts altogether. Instead, they're about navigating them with grace, ensuring your relationships remain strong and fulfilling. As you move forward, consider how emotional intelligence can enrich your connections, paving the way for deeper understanding and mutual respect. Next, we'll explore how to celebrate love in meaningful ways that go beyond material gestures.

7

Chapter 7: Celebrating Love Without Cost

Picture this: you're at your favourite café, and across the room, a young woman is reading a book. She suddenly puts it down, pulls out a small piece of paper, and starts writing. Her eyes light up as she scribbles, folds the note, and tucks it into her bag. It's a simple act, but one that holds a universe of possibilities. Maybe she's crafting a heartfelt letter for a friend, a note of gratitude for her partner, or perhaps a reminder of love to herself. This moment captures the magic of expressing love without spending a dime—a theme we'll explore deeply in this chapter.

In a world that often equates love with material gifts, it's refreshing to remember the power of small gestures. You know, those little acts that say, "I care" without needing to swipe a card. Writing a personalised poem or letter is one such gesture. Imagine receiving a handwritten letter filled with words that speak directly to your soul. It's like getting a warm hug through paper and ink. A few heartfelt lines about shared memories or future dreams can mean more than any store-bought card. And these gestures are not just for romantic partners—they're for friends, family, or anyone who holds a special place in your heart.

Another way to express love without cost is through creating handmade gifts using materials you have at home. It could be as simple as crafting a photo album with printed pictures and little notes beside them. Or maybe you knit a scarf, bake some cookies, or create a playlist with songs that hold special meaning. The effort and thought behind these gifts make them priceless. They show that you're willing to invest time and creativity, which speaks volumes about how much you cherish the relationship.

Acts of service are another profound way to communicate love. Think about the last time someone cooked your favourite meal or helped with chores you were dreading. Cooking a meal together, for instance, can be a delightful way to bond. It's about the shared experience, the laughter over a failed recipe, or the joy of discovering a new favourite dish. Offering to take on chores to lighten a partner's load isn't just about getting things done— it's about saying, "I'm here for you." These acts are practical expressions of love, showing that you're willing to support and care for one another in tangible ways.

Words, too, are powerful conveyors of love. Expressing gratitude and admiration doesn't require a special occasion. Try telling your loved ones what you appreciate about them out of the blue. "I'm so grateful for your support," or "Your smile makes my day brighter," can turn an ordinary day into something special. Sharing affirmations and positive reflections can also uplift and strengthen bonds. It's about acknowledging the little things and cherishing each other's presence in your lives. Words can heal, inspire, and connect, making them one of the most accessible ways to express love.

Physical affection is another beautiful, non-material way to show love. A warm hug at the end of a long day can convey more than words ever could. Hugs release feel-good hormones like dopamine, serotonin, and oxytocin, which help build emotional connections and reduce stress. Holding hands during a walk in the park, or even just sitting close while watching a movie, can nurture intimacy and closeness. These small gestures affirm that you're there, offering comfort and companionship without needing to say a word.

Interactive Element: Love Language Exploration

Take a moment to reflect on your preferred love language. Do you resonate more with words of affirmation, acts of service, physical touch, quality time, or receiving gifts? Consider how you express love to others and how you feel most loved in return. Write a short reflection on what each love language means to you and how you might incorporate more non-material expressions of love into your relationships. This exercise can enhance your understanding of how love is felt and shared in your life.

In celebrating love without cost, we uncover the richness of relationships built on genuine connection and care. It's about the shared moments, the thoughtful gestures, and the heartfelt words that weave a tapestry of love. These expressions are accessible to everyone, regardless of financial means, and they remind us that love, at its core, is about presence, intention, and authenticity.

Creating Meaningful Memories Together

Imagine stepping onto a fresh hiking trail, the air crisp and the path winding through a canopy of vibrant leaves. It's just you and someone special, each step creating a new memory etched into the landscape of your relationship. Exploring a new hiking trail offers more than just exercise; it's an adventure that strengthens bonds. As you navigate the twists and turns, you share stories, laugh at the occasional misstep, and perhaps even find a secret spot to sit and enjoy the view. These shared experiences become the foundation of your connection, creating a tapestry of memories that enrich your relationship. Similarly, having a picnic in the backyard can transform an ordinary afternoon into a cherished moment. Spread a blanket, pack some sandwiches, and let the simplicity of the setting foster conversation and laughter. Whether you're watching clouds drift by or sharing your dreams for the future, these small adventures bring you closer together, one memory at a time.

Sometimes, the most memorable moments are born out of creativity and spontaneity. Picture this: it's a chilly evening, and you've decided to build a blanket fort in the living room. Pillows are piled high, fairy lights twinkle above, and a cosy movie night awaits. Inside that makeshift haven, you and your loved one find warmth and comfort, sharing popcorn and laughter as the movie plays in the background. These creative endeavours break the routine, adding a touch of magic to everyday life. Or imagine a clear night sky, dotted with stars. You lay side by side, bundled up in blankets, discussing dreams and wondering about the universe. Stargazing becomes a canvas for imagination, where dreams are painted in constellations and whispered into the night. These activities aren't about grand gestures; they're about creating spaces where connection and joy flourish naturally.

In today's digital age, technology offers us tools to capture and preserve these precious moments. Creating a digital photo album of shared experiences is like curating a gallery of your relationship's highlights. Each photo tells a story, from the first selfie on a spontaneous road trip to candid shots of everyday joys. As you flip through the album, you relive the laughter, the adventures, and the love that fills each frame. Similarly, recording a video diary of special days together allows you to capture the essence of each experience, preserving the sights and sounds that make them unforgettable. These digital mementos become time capsules, allowing you to revisit and cherish the memories long after the moment has passed.

Spontaneity is the spice of life, and in relationships, it adds a dash of excitement and unpredictability. Imagine deciding on a whim to take a road trip to a nearby town you've never explored. The thrill of the unknown, the unexpected detours, and the discoveries you make along the way create memories that are uniquely yours. It's not about the destination; it's about the journey, the shared laughter, and the sense of adventure. Or picture dancing together to your favourite songs in the living room, the world outside fading away as the music fills the air. These spontaneous moments, unplanned and unscripted, become the stories you tell, the ones that remind you of the joy and freedom of simply being together.

Creating meaningful memories together isn't about the grandeur of the moment but the depth of the connection. It's the shared experiences, the laughter, and the love that leave a lasting imprint on your hearts. Whether you're exploring new places, building blanket forts, capturing memories with technology, or embracing spontaneity, each moment becomes a thread in the tapestry of your relationship. These memories are treasures, reminders of the love and joy that fill your lives. As you create these moments, you also create a legacy of love, a story that's uniquely yours, filled with adventures, laughter, and the beauty of simply being together.

Celebrating Anniversaries with Thoughtfulness

Anniversaries, those special markers of time in a relationship, often come with the expectation of grand gestures and expensive gifts. But what if we reimagined these celebrations as intimate occasions, focusing on the depth of the bond rather than its price tag? Picture this: you and your partner decide to recreate your first date at home. Maybe it was a cosy coffee shop where you shared your first awkward yet adorable conversation over lattes. Now, you transform your living room into that very scene, complete with homemade coffee and your favourite playlist softly playing in the background. As you reminisce about those early days, you realise it's the shared laughter and the stories that make this moment special, bringing you back to the roots of your connection.

Another heartfelt way to celebrate is to sit down and write a list of reasons why you love your partner. It's a simple yet profound exercise that allows you to reflect on what makes your relationship unique. Maybe it's their quirky sense of humour that never fails to make you smile, or the way they support your dreams without hesitation. As you jot down each reason, you're reminded of the little things that often go unnoticed but mean the world. Sharing this list with your partner can be a deeply moving experience, one that strengthens your bond and rekindles the spark that brought you together in the first place.

Establishing thoughtful rituals for anniversaries can also add a meaningful layer to your celebrations. Consider exchanging heartfelt letters each year, where you express your hopes, dreams, and gratitude. These letters become treasured keepsakes, capturing the essence of your relationship as it evolves over time. Another beautiful ritual is planting a tree or flower together, symbolising the growth and resilience of your relationship. With each passing year, as the plant flourishes, it serves as a living reminder of your commitment to nurturing and supporting one another through life's seasons.

Taking the time to reflect on your relationship's growth is an invaluable practice. Set aside moments to discuss the journey you've travelled together, acknowledging shared achievements and milestones. Whether it's overcoming challenges, supporting each other's ambitions, or simply being there through the everyday ups and downs, these reflections reinforce the strength of your partnership. Looking back at photos or videos from past anniversaries can also be a delightful trip down memory lane, evoking laughter and nostalgia as you relive cherished moments.

Creating personal traditions that hold special significance for you both adds a unique touch to your anniversaries. One idea is to create a time capsule together, filling it with mementos, letters, and predictions for the future. Seal it away and plan to open it on a future anniversary, allowing you to reflect on how far you've come and how much you've grown. Another tradition could be cooking a new dish together each year. With each attempt, whether it's a culinary triumph or a hilarious disaster, you're making memories and embracing the unpredictable nature of life and love.

Anniversaries offer a chance to pause and celebrate the love that has grown between you, not through lavish gifts, but through thoughtful gestures and meaningful traditions that reflect the depth of your connection. Each celebration becomes a chapter in your love story, adding richness and texture to the tapestry of your relationship. The focus shifts from impressing one another to appreciating the journey you share, finding joy in the simple act of being together. Through these thoughtful celebrations, you honour the past, embrace the present, and look forward to the future with hope and excitement.

The Joy of Shared Experiences

Imagine coming home after a hectic day, the world still buzzing in your mind, and then stepping into a space filled with calm and connection. It's your regular date night, a cherished ritual where the outside world fades away, leaving just the two of you. Whether it's cooking a meal together, playing a favourite board game, or simply lounging on the couch watching a beloved show, these moments are golden. They're not just about being in the same room; they're about being truly present with each other. This intentional quality time is like a balm for busy lives, creating a sanctuary where you can both recharge and reconnect. Engaging in a mutual hobby, whether it's painting, gardening, or even something quirky like learning to juggle, adds another layer to this connection. Sharing interests not only strengthens your bond but also brings joy and laughter into your life, reminding you of the simple pleasures of being together.

Nature offers a breathtaking backdrop for connection. Picture a scenic walk, the path lined with trees whispering secrets to the wind, or a hike up a gentle hill where the view is a sprawling tapestry of greens and blues. These natural settings have a way of stripping away distractions, leaving room for genuine conversation and shared wonder. There's something magical about watching a sunrise paint the sky in hues of pink and orange, or witnessing a sunset as it casts a golden glow over everything. These moments in nature allow you to pause, breathe, and appreciate the beauty around you and in each other. It's a reminder that sometimes the most profound connections happen when you step away from the hustle and bustle and immerse yourselves in the simplicity and grandeur of the natural world. Whether you're sharing awe at the vastness of the sky or just enjoying the quiet of each other's company, nature becomes a canvas for heartfelt connection.

Collaborating on shared projects can be a delightful way to bond. Imagine starting a garden together, your hands digging into the earth as you plant seeds that will one day bloom into vibrant flowers or tasty vegetables. It's a labour of love, requiring patience and care, much like a relationship itself. As you water and tend to your garden, you're also nurturing your connection, watching it grow and flourish over time. Or consider tackling a DIY project, transforming a piece of furniture or redecorating a room. The shared effort and teamwork involved can be incredibly satisfying, creating a sense of accomplishment and unity. Volunteering together for a cause you both care about is another wonderful option. Whether it's helping out at a local shelter or participating in a community clean-up, giving back can strengthen your bond and provide a shared sense of purpose, reminding you of the impact you can have when you work together.

Learning something new as a couple is an exciting way to foster growth and connection. Envision signing up for an online class, perhaps in a subject neither of you knows much about—like cooking a foreign cuisine, mastering a new language, or even trying your hand at digital photography. The process of learning together brings fresh energy into your relationship, sparking curiosity and creativity. It's a journey of discovery, where you can encourage each other's progress and celebrate small victories along the way. Reading and discussing the same book can also offer a rich avenue for connection. Imagine curling up with a novel or a thought-provoking non-fiction piece, then coming together to share your thoughts, insights, and different perspectives. These discussions can deepen your understanding of each other, revealing facets of your partner's mind that you might not have seen before. Through learning, you not only expand your horizons but also weave new threads into the fabric of your relationship, creating a tapestry of shared knowledge and experiences.

Spending meaningful time together, whether rooted in nature, shared projects, or new learning experiences, enriches your connection and adds depth to your relationship. These moments, both grand and simple, remind you of the joy in companionship and the beauty of growing together. As we look ahead, the next chapter will delve into diverse perspectives on love, exploring how different cultural and personal backgrounds shape our understanding and expression of this timeless emotion.

8

Chapter 8: Diverse Perspectives on Love

Imagine stepping into a bustling market, vibrant colours swirling around you, and the air filled with the chatter of countless languages. Each stall holds treasures from different lands, each vendor a storyteller with tales of love that span continents and centuries. Love, like a universal language, transcends borders, yet it's expressed uniquely across cultures. From the whispered words of a Japanese lover to the rhythmic beats of African drums at a wedding, the way love is celebrated around the world is as diverse as it is beautiful. These traditions not only reflect the customs of a culture but also the values that hold love together, binding people in ways that are both familiar and new. For instance, in Japan, the concept of "amae," which means depending on another's kindness, highlights the gentle give-and-take that forms the backbone of many relationships. This reliance fosters a deep bond, emphasising love as a nurturing force rather than a transaction.

Meanwhile, in India, the tradition of arranged marriages might seem like an odd dance to those in the West, but it's a celebration of familial bonds and community. Here, love often grows after marriage, nurtured by the commitment of not just the couple but their families. It's an intricate tapestry woven with respect and dedication, where love is seen as a lifelong partnership rather than a fleeting romance. In contrast, consider the Sisters' Meal Festival in China, a lively tradition where single men court women through the artful exchange of dyed rice. Hidden messages in the rice speak of intentions and emotions, turning a simple meal into a language of love. Each of these practices, though distinct, shares a common thread—the desire to connect deeply and authentically with another, transcending the chaos of modern life.

Across cultures, universal themes of love emerge, such as commitment, respect, and loyalty. These values form the core of relationships, acting as the glue that holds them together. Loyalty, in particular, is a universal value cherished across cultures—a promise to stand by each other through thick and thin, reflecting the heart of what it means to truly love someone. Whether it's in the quiet devotion of a lifelong partner or the fierce loyalty of a best friend, this theme resonates universally. It's like the tale of Romeo and Juliet or Layla and Majnun, lovers separated by fate yet bound by unyielding devotion. Their stories remind us that love's power lies not in its grand gestures but in the steadfast commitment to one another, even when the world stands against you.

Cultural stories and legends have long served as vessels for these themes, passing down wisdom from one generation to the next. In Morocco, the Imilchil Marriage Festival commemorates a tragic love story, allowing men and women to choose their partners freely as a tribute to those who dared to love beyond societal constraints. Such tales celebrate love's enduring power and its ability to transcend time and tradition. Whether it's the Zulu girls of South Africa using courting huts for secret meetings or the Wodaabe people of Niger celebrating beauty in their unique way, each narrative adds a rich layer to the global tapestry of love. These stories are not just tales of romance; they are reflections of cultural values, illustrating how love adapts to the norms and beliefs of each society.

The influence of culture on relationship dynamics is profound, shaping how individuals approach love and connection. In Latin cultures, familial expectations often play a significant role in relationships, where the family is seen as an integral part of the partnership. This community-centric view fosters a sense of belonging and support, emphasising the importance of family unity in love. Similarly, in many African traditions, community plays a pivotal role, with relationships often seen within the broader context of communal ties. This perspective highlights the idea that love is not just between two people but a bond that enriches the entire community. It's a reminder that while love is deeply personal, it's also a shared experience, touching the lives of many.

Reflection Section: Cultural Love Traditions

Take a moment to reflect on a love tradition from your own culture. How does it shape your view of relationships? Perhaps there's a family tradition or cultural practice you hold dear. Write it down and consider sharing it with someone you care about. Discuss how these traditions influence your understanding of love and connection. This reflection can deepen your appreciation for the diverse ways love is celebrated around the world, highlighting the common threads that unite us all.

Inclusivity in Love: Embracing Diversity

Inclusivity in relationships means more than just acknowledging differences; it's about embracing them wholeheartedly. It's about creating a space where all identities and orientations are not just accepted but celebrated. This inclusivity is crucial because love is not one-size-fits-all. It wears many faces and speaks in myriad tongues. For those exploring different sexual orientations and identities, inclusivity becomes a sanctuary where love is free to express itself in its truest form. Imagine the freedom of loving who you choose without fear of judgement or rejection. This acceptance transforms relationships into vibrant tapestries, each thread adding depth and colour.

Consider the stories of interracial couples who navigate the complex dance of cultural differences. These relationships often face challenges that others might not, like balancing diverse traditions or confronting societal biases. Yet, they also offer a unique richness, a blending of worlds that creates something entirely new. Each partner brings their heritage, their customs, and their perspectives, weaving them together into a love story that defies conventional norms. It's like a culinary fusion, where diverse ingredients come together to create a dish that's both novel and familiar. The beauty lies in the harmony of differences, in the shared journey of discovery and understanding.

LGBTQ+ relationships, too, embody the spirit of inclusivity. They challenge traditional norms and stereotypes, offering a glimpse into the diverse expressions of love that exist beyond the binary. These relationships often face unique challenges, from societal stigma to legal hurdles. However, they also demonstrate incredible resilience and pride. The strength of these connections lies in their authenticity and the courage to love openly in a world that sometimes struggles to understand. It's a powerful reminder that love knows no boundaries, that it thrives in every corner of the human experience, regardless of gender or orientation. The resilience shown by LGBTQ+ couples can inspire all of us to embrace love in its many forms.

Diversity in relationships enriches our lives, offering exposure to different worldviews and customs. It's like opening a window to the world, allowing fresh air and new perspectives to flow in. When you engage with someone from a different background, you embark on a journey of exploration and growth. You learn to appreciate the richness of their culture, their history, and their experiences. This exposure broadens your horizons, challenging preconceived notions and encouraging personal growth. It's like travelling without leaving home, a passport to understanding humanity in all its diversity. The more you learn, the more you realise that despite our differences, we all share the same fundamental desire to love and be loved.

To embrace diversity in your relationships, it's important to actively learn about your partner's cultural background. This effort demonstrates respect and a willingness to understand their world. It's like learning a new language, where each phrase and gesture opens up new layers of meaning. Ask questions, listen to stories, and participate in cultural traditions. This active engagement fosters a deeper connection and enriches your shared experiences. Practising empathy and open-mindedness in discussions is equally crucial. Approach conversations with curiosity and a genuine desire to learn. This openness creates a safe space where both partners feel valued and understood, paving the way for honest and meaningful exchanges.

Celebrating diversity in love involves more than just acceptance; it requires active participation and understanding. It's about recognizing that each relationship is a unique dance, with its own rhythm and steps. By embracing diversity, you enrich your life and the lives of those you love. This inclusivity fosters an environment where love can flourish in all its forms, free from the constraints of societal norms or expectations. It's a celebration of the human experience, a testament to the beauty of love in all its diversity. As you navigate your own relationships, remember that every connection offers an opportunity to learn, grow, and discover the endless possibilities that love holds.

Learning from Different Relationship Models

Love doesn't come with a one-size-fits-all label. It wears many hats, each as unique as the people who choose to wear them. In recent years, there has been a growing interest in exploring relationship models beyond the conventional. Polyamory, for instance, challenges the traditional notion of monogamy by embracing multiple consensual relationships. Imagine a circle of partners, each with their own connections and dynamics, yet all united by mutual respect and understanding. This model thrives on communication, trust, and the ability to navigate complex emotions. It asks for honesty and openness, teaching us that love doesn't have to be limited to one person. There's beauty in knowing that love can be abundant and shared freely without diminishing its value.

Another fascinating model is communal living arrangements, where a group of people shares their lives in a close-knit community. This isn't just about splitting rent; it's about creating a support network where relationships go beyond romantic ties. In such settings, love is a shared experience, where friendships and family-like bonds form the core of daily life. Picture a household where meals are communal, decisions are collective, and support is always at hand. This model emphasises collaboration, empathy, and the understanding that love can thrive in a multitude of forms. It challenges the notion that romantic love is the pinnacle of relationships, reminding us that deep connections can be found in the bonds we build with those around us.

When you look back at historical relationship models, you see a tapestry of traditions and practices that have evolved over time. Take the courting practices of the Victorian era, where love was a carefully orchestrated dance of letters, chaperoned meetings, and whispered affections. This era placed a premium on propriety and restraint, viewing love as a gradual unfolding rather than a whirlwind romance. Fast forward to modern times, and you'll find millennials redefining relationships through cohabitation and less traditional commitments. Living together before marriage, or even without the intent to marry, reflects a shift toward valuing shared experiences and compatibility over societal expectations. This modern approach emphasises the importance of partnership and shared growth, free from the constraints of formal institutions.

Love's adaptability is one of its most remarkable qualities. It can mould itself to fit various relationship models, each unique in its own right. Emotional support networks, often seen in chosen families, highlight how love transcends biological ties. These families are built on the foundation of shared values, mutual care, and chosen connections. They remind us that family is not solely determined by blood but by the bonds we choose to nurture. In these networks, love is a deliberate choice, offering support and belonging in a world that can sometimes feel isolating. It teaches us that love is not limited by traditional structures but is expansive and inclusive, embracing all who seek it.

Unconventional relationship models offer valuable lessons for anyone willing to explore them. Clear communication and boundaries are essential, ensuring that everyone involved understands and respects each other's needs and expectations. This is true for any relationship, but it becomes even more crucial when multiple partners or communal living is involved. It's about having honest conversations, addressing concerns, and setting boundaries that create a safe and respectful environment for everyone. Balancing autonomy with commitment is another lesson that stands out. Whether in a polyamorous relationship or a communal living arrangement, the ability to maintain individuality while committing to a shared life is key. It's like walking a tightrope, balancing personal freedom with the shared responsibilities of a collective relationship.

These models encourage us to think outside the box, to question societal norms, and to find what truly works for us. They remind us that love is as diverse as the people who experience it, and there is no single path to happiness. Each relationship, whether traditional or unconventional, offers opportunities for growth, understanding, and connection. By embracing these varied models, we open ourselves to new possibilities, expanding our understanding of what love can be. It's an invitation to explore, learn, and redefine relationships on our own terms.

The Universal Language of Emotional Connection

Love speaks many languages, but the most profound among them is emotional connection—a form of communication that transcends words and cultural barriers. It's fascinating how a simple gesture, like a warm smile or a comforting touch, can convey volumes about what we feel inside. Nonverbal cues such as these create an unspoken dialogue, a universal language that all humans understand. Imagine sitting beside someone who is hurting. You might not know their language, but holding their hand or offering a gentle nod can express empathy and support. This silent communication forms the foundation of emotional bonds, regardless of where you come from or what language you speak.

The formation of emotional connections is a complex dance of psychological and emotional processes. When two people share an experience, whether it's a moment of joy or a challenging ordeal, they lay the groundwork for a deeper bond. These shared experiences act as threads woven into the fabric of a relationship, creating a tapestry rich with mutual understanding and trust. For instance, working through a group project or overcoming a crisis together can strengthen ties by fostering a sense of unity and cooperation. It's these moments of shared triumph and struggle that cement emotional connections, making them strong enough to withstand the tests of time and circumstance.

Consider the stories of international couples who manage to thrive despite the cultural and linguistic chasms they must bridge. Their relationships often start with curiosity and fascination, but they require more than just attraction to endure. These couples learn to navigate their differences, finding common ground in shared values and emotional goals. One might be from a bustling city in Japan, the other from a quiet village in Italy, yet their love speaks the same language. By embracing each other's cultures, they enrich their bond with diverse perspectives and experiences. It's like a beautiful duet where each voice complements the other, creating harmony from diversity. This mutual respect and understanding allow love to flourish, proving that emotional connection can conquer even the widest of gaps.

Strengthening emotional bonds requires intention and effort, but the rewards are immeasurable. One effective strategy is practising active listening, which involves truly hearing what the other person is saying without preparing your response while they speak. This level of attention shows that you value their thoughts and feelings, fostering a deeper connection. Coupled with empathy, which involves putting yourself in someone else's shoes, active listening can transform ordinary interactions into meaningful exchanges. These practices help build trust, as they demonstrate a genuine interest in understanding and supporting each other.

Engaging in shared activities is another powerful way to enhance emotional connections. Whether it's cooking a meal together, taking a dance class, or simply going for a walk, these moments create opportunities for bonding and building trust. They provide a space where both parties can be themselves, free from judgement or expectation. Through these experiences, you learn more about each other, discovering new facets and shared interests. It's like opening a book and finding new chapters that you never knew existed, adding depth and richness to your relationship. These activities not only strengthen existing bonds but also lay the foundation for future connections, ensuring that love continues to grow and evolve.

The beauty of emotional connection lies in its ability to transcend boundaries, uniting people from different backgrounds in a shared understanding of love. As you explore these connections, you'll find that love's language is universal, capable of bridging any divide. This chapter invites you to embrace the power of emotional bonds, recognizing their role in creating meaningful and lasting relationships. Whether through a gentle touch, a shared laugh, or a heartfelt conversation, emotional connections offer a path to deeper, more fulfilling relationships. As we move forward, let's continue to explore the myriad ways love can manifest, enriching our lives and the lives of those around us.

9

Chapter 9: Inner Dialogue and Reflection

Picture this: you're standing in front of the mirror, staring at your reflection as you get ready for a day that promises its usual ups and downs. You notice a stray hair out of place, and before you know it, a tiny voice in your head whispers, "You really should have fixed that." This is your inner dialogue—the ongoing conversation you have with yourself, shaping how you perceive the world and interact with it. It's like a personal narrator, sometimes helpful, other times not so much. This internal conversation can be your best friend or your worst critic, influencing your actions, decisions, and relationships in ways you might not even realise.

Inner dialogue comes in two flavours: positive and negative self-talk. Positive self-talk is like having a supportive cheerleader inside your mind—encouraging, uplifting, and ready to remind you of your strengths. It's the voice that says, "You've got this," when you're faced with a challenge or "It's okay, everyone makes mistakes," when things don't go as planned. On the flip side, negative self-talk resembles a pesky critic, always ready to point out flaws and shortcomings. It's the voice that says, "You'll never be good enough," or "Why even bother trying?" These negative messages can erode your self-esteem and affect how you perceive your relationships, leaving you feeling inadequate or unworthy of love.

The impact of inner dialogue on your relationships is profound. When your internal conversation leans towards negativity, it can shape how you respond to conflicts and interact with your partner. If you're constantly telling yourself that you're not good enough or that your partner doesn't really care, you'll likely approach disagreements with defensiveness or withdrawal. This can create a cycle where your partner feels unheard or misunderstood, further straining the relationship. On the other hand, a positive inner dialogue fosters open communication and empathy, allowing you to approach conflicts with a willingness to understand and resolve issues collaboratively.

Expectations in relationships are often shaped by inner dialogue. If your self-talk is filled with doubt and insecurity, you might expect your partner to constantly reassure you, creating pressure and tension. However, when your inner dialogue is supportive, you feel more secure in your relationship, reducing the need for external validation. You trust in the strength of your connection and approach your partner with confidence and openness, enhancing the bond between you. This shift in perspective allows you to focus on the positive aspects of your relationship, fostering a deeper sense of connection and trust.

Improving your inner dialogue requires practice, but it's a journey worth embarking on. Mindfulness is a powerful tool for becoming aware of your thoughts and recognizing patterns of negative self-talk. By observing your thoughts without judgement, you can start to notice when your inner critic takes over and gently redirect your focus. Replacing negative self-statements with affirmations is another effective strategy. Instead of saying, "I'm such a failure," try saying, "I am learning and growing every day." These affirmations act as gentle reminders of your worth and potential, gradually reshaping your internal narrative.

The benefits of cultivating a positive inner dialogue extend far beyond your relationship with yourself. When you approach your interactions with greater confidence, you naturally express your needs and desires with clarity and assertiveness. This openness fosters honest communication and mutual understanding, strengthening the foundation of your relationship. Reduced anxiety and increased emotional stability also result from a positive inner dialogue, allowing you to navigate challenges with grace and resilience. You become more adaptable and less reactive, fostering a more harmonious and fulfilling partnership.

Interactive Element: Crafting Personal Affirmations

To help shift your inner dialogue towards positivity, try crafting a list of personal affirmations. These are short, empowering statements that reflect your values and aspirations. For example, "I am deserving of love and respect," or "I approach challenges with courage and curiosity." Write them down and place them somewhere visible, like your mirror or journal. Repeat these affirmations daily, allowing them to reinforce your inner dialogue and remind you of your inherent worth. As you incorporate this practice into your routine, notice how your perspective shifts and how it influences your interactions with others.

Reflecting on Personal Values in Relationships

Imagine you're standing at a crossroads, trying to decide which path to take. Each path represents a choice in your life, shaped by your personal values. These values act like a compass, guiding you through the maze of decisions, especially in relationships. They are the principles that define who you are and what you stand for. When you understand your core values, like integrity and compassion, you can navigate relationships with a clarity that helps you stay true to yourself. Integrity, for instance, isn't just about being honest with others; it's about being honest with yourself. It means aligning your actions with your beliefs, even when it's difficult. Compassion, on the other hand, is the lens through which you view and interact with those around you. It's about empathy, kindness, and understanding, creating a nurturing environment where love can thrive.

Discovering your personal values is a bit like digging for treasure—sometimes you have to sift through the sand to find the gems. A good place to start is by writing a value inventory. This exercise involves listing the values that resonate most with you. Consider what makes you feel proud, fulfilled, and content. Think about moments when you've felt most aligned with yourself. What values were you honouring at those times? Reflecting on past decisions can also offer insights into your values. Consider choices you've made that left you feeling satisfied or, conversely, those that led to regret. These reflections can shed light on the values that guide you, even if unconsciously.

Once you've identified your personal values, aligning them with your relationship dynamics can lead to harmony and fulfillment. When partners share common values, mutual respect forms the foundation of the relationship. It's like building a house on solid ground; everything feels more stable and secure. Shared values foster a sense of unity and understanding, where both partners are moving towards the same goals. They act as a guide in navigating conflicts, helping you find solutions that honour both your perspectives. Imagine a couple who values honesty above all else. When disagreements arise, they approach them with openness and transparency, knowing that their shared value will guide them towards resolution.

Making relationship decisions that honour your personal values can be challenging, but it's incredibly rewarding. Start by setting relationship goals that reflect these values. If growth and learning are important to you, create goals that encourage both partners to pursue personal development and support each other's aspirations. This can involve activities like taking a class together or setting aside time for self-reflection. Evaluating relationship conflicts through the lens of your values can also be enlightening. When you find yourself in a disagreement, pause and consider how your values play into the situation. Are you honouring them, or are they being compromised? This reflection can offer clarity and help you approach the conflict with empathy and understanding.

Aligning values doesn't mean you and your partner must agree on everything, but it does mean you respect each other's differences and find common ground. It's about creating a partnership where both individuals feel valued and understood. When values are out of alignment, misunderstandings and resentments can build. It's like trying to drive a car with wheels that aren't aligned—eventually, something will give. By prioritising shared values, you build a relationship that not only withstands challenges but thrives in the face of them. Values become the glue that holds the relationship together, providing a sense of purpose and direction.

Reflecting on and honouring your personal values in relationships can transform how you connect with others. It encourages you to live authentically, making choices that resonate with who you truly are. This authenticity fosters deeper, more meaningful connections, where both partners feel empowered to be themselves. As you continue to explore and refine your values, remember that they are not set in stone. They can evolve over time, just as you do. Embrace this evolution, and let your values guide you towards relationships that enrich your life and reflect your true self.

Journaling for Emotional Clarity

Imagine sitting down at the end of a long day, your mind a whirlwind of thoughts and emotions. You grab a notebook and pen, ready to pour your heart onto its pages. This is journaling—a reflective practice that offers a window into your inner world. It's like having a conversation with yourself, one that can lead to profound insights and self-awareness. Through journaling, you capture your daily thoughts and feelings, creating a space to process experiences and navigate the complexities of life. It's a place to explore your emotions without fear of judgement, where you can be raw and honest, uncovering truths that might otherwise remain hidden.

To make the most of journaling, consider different techniques that can enhance your self-reflection and insight. One approach is stream-of-consciousness writing, where you let your thoughts flow freely onto the page without worrying about structure or grammar. This can be incredibly liberating, allowing you to tap into your subconscious and uncover patterns or themes you hadn't noticed before. Another effective method is prompt-based journaling, where specific topics guide your writing. Prompts can help focus your thoughts and encourage deeper exploration of particular areas, such as "What am I grateful for today?" or "What challenges did I face, and how did I overcome them?" These techniques create a structured yet flexible framework that encourages introspection and growth.

Journaling can profoundly impact your relationships by enhancing understanding and communication. As you write about your interactions and experiences, you may identify recurring emotional patterns that influence how you relate to others. Perhaps you notice a tendency to withdraw during conflicts or a habit of seeking reassurance when feeling insecure. Recognizing these patterns allows you to address them consciously, leading to more intentional and constructive interactions with your partner. By understanding your emotional landscape, you can communicate your needs and feelings more effectively, fostering a deeper connection and mutual understanding.

To facilitate introspection and growth, try incorporating specific journaling exercises into your routine. Reflecting on a recent conflict and the lessons learned can be incredibly insightful. Consider what triggered the disagreement, how you felt, and how you might approach similar situations differently in the future. This reflection can illuminate underlying issues and provide clarity on how to navigate challenges more effectively. Exploring personal fears and aspirations is another valuable exercise. By examining what holds you back and what drives you forward, you gain a better understanding of your motivations and desires. This awareness empowers you to make choices that align with your true self, both in your relationships and personal life.

Journaling is a versatile and accessible tool that can support emotional clarity and self-awareness. It's a space where you can explore your inner world, gain insights into your thoughts and feelings, and navigate the complexities of life and relationships with greater understanding and intention. As you continue to journal, you may find that this practice becomes a trusted companion, offering guidance and support as you navigate the ups and downs of life's journey.

Self-Talk as a Tool for Relationship Growth

Imagine your mind as a constant chatterbox, always buzzing with an inner dialogue that guides your actions and feelings. This is self-talk, the ongoing dialogue within yourself that profoundly affects your self-esteem and how you interact in relationships. It's like having an ever-present narrator, sometimes supportive, other times critical, influencing how you perceive both yourself and others. Self-talk can be a powerful tool, either bolstering your confidence or undermining your sense of worth. Understanding its influence can help you navigate relationships with greater confidence and clarity.

Self-talk comes in three main flavours: positive, negative, and neutral. Positive self-talk is your inner cheerleader, offering encouragement and reminding you of your strengths. It's the voice that tells you, "You can do this," or "You're doing great." This type of dialogue boosts your confidence and resilience, helping you face challenges with optimism. On the opposite end, negative self-talk acts like a harsh critic, always pointing out flaws and predicting failure. It whispers things like, "You'll never get it right," or "No one really cares." These self-critical statements can erode self-esteem and foster insecurity, making it difficult to trust in your own abilities or the intentions of others. Then there's neutral self-talk, which observes without judgement. It simply notes facts without attaching emotions, like saying to yourself, "I'm feeling tired," without adding a layer of criticism or praise. This type of self-talk can be grounding, offering a balanced perspective when emotions run high.

So, how can you cultivate a more positive self-talk? One effective method is to reframe negative thoughts into constructive feedback. When you catch yourself thinking, "I messed up," try shifting it to, "I learned something valuable from this experience." This simple act of rephrasing can transform self-criticism into an opportunity for growth and reflection. Another strategy involves practising self-compassion. When you speak to yourself with kindness and understanding, you create a nurturing internal environment. Imagine how you would comfort a friend going through a tough time, and extend that same compassion to yourself. By treating yourself with the same empathy you offer others, you can gradually replace harsh self-talk with a dialogue that supports and empowers.

The benefits of fostering positive self-talk ripple through every aspect of your life, enhancing both personal and relational growth. When you speak to yourself with kindness, your self-esteem and confidence naturally improve. You start to believe in your abilities and trust in your instincts, which can lead to more assertive and effective communication in relationships. This increased confidence allows you to express your needs and desires openly, fostering a deeper connection with your partner. Positive self-talk also bolsters resilience, helping you navigate relationship challenges with grace and composure. Instead of succumbing to feelings of inadequacy or fear, you approach conflicts with a sense of calm and clarity, ready to find solutions and growth opportunities.

As you nurture a positive self-talk habit, you might notice a shift in your perspective. Challenges become less daunting, and setbacks are seen as stepping stones rather than roadblocks. This mindset not only enriches your relationship with yourself but also enhances your interactions with others. You begin to see your partner through a lens of empathy and understanding, recognizing that they, too, have their own inner dialogue. This awareness fosters mutual respect and support, creating a relationship dynamic that thrives on shared growth and love.

In the next chapter, we'll explore how these internal conversations, combined with understanding others' perspectives, can lead to deeper connections and more fulfilling relationships. Let's keep this momentum going as we continue to delve into the power of love and connection.

10

Chapter 10: Inspirational Journeys and Endings

Close your eyes for a moment and picture a couple in a small, sunlit kitchen. They're dancing to an old song on the radio, laughing as they step on each other's toes. There's no fancy furniture or expensive gadgets, just two people wrapped in each other's arms, lost in the moment. This couple, Jane and Mark, chose emotional support over financial success. They met in college, both juggling part-time jobs and ramen dinners. Instead of dreaming of a mansion, they dreamed of a life filled with simple joys. Their turning point came when they decided to invest in each other's dreams rather than chase material wealth. Jane wanted to write, and Mark longed to teach. Supporting each other, they built a life where success wasn't measured by a paycheck but by the fulfillment of their passions and the depth of their love.

In another tale, the Martinez family found unity through shared values rather than wealth. Growing up, they didn't have much. Their living room was filled with mismatched furniture, but it was always full of laughter and warmth. Every Sunday, they gathered for a family meal, a tradition that became the highlight of their week. It wasn't about what was on the table but who was around it. The turning point came when they decided to prioritise these gatherings over any material gifts during the holidays. This choice strengthened their bond, teaching them that what truly mattered was the time spent together. Their unity became a source of strength, weathering any storm life threw their way.

These stories illustrate the profound impact of choosing love over materialism. Jane and Mark's decision to prioritise experiences over possessions led to a life of shared adventures and mutual growth. Their love story is a testament that fulfillment often lies in the journey, not the destination. The Martinez family, by focusing on values and traditions, discovered that true wealth isn't found in bank accounts but in the memories and the love they share.

Reflection Section: Personal Story Inventory

Think about your own life and the relationships that have shaped you. Are there moments where you chose connection over material things? What traditions or experiences bring you joy and fulfillment? Take a few minutes to jot down these memories. Consider how these choices have enriched your life and what they reveal about your values. This reflection can serve as a reminder of what truly matters and guide you toward nurturing deeper connections in the future.

10.2 Lessons from Inspirational Love Journeys

In the stories of love that defy materialism, resilience emerges as a key player. It's like the friend who sticks by you when times get tough, offering a shoulder to lean on. Resilience isn't about avoiding challenges; it's about facing them head-on, knowing that each hurdle is an opportunity for growth. Imagine a couple navigating the choppy waters of financial difficulty. Instead of letting the stress pull them apart, they band together, turning obstacles into stepping stones. They learn to communicate better, budget wisely, and prioritise their emotional connection over material desires. This resilience not only strengthens their bond but also teaches them to appreciate the simple joys in life, like a quiet evening spent together or a walk in the park.

Patience and perseverance are like the unsung heroes in these relationships. They're the quiet forces that keep love alive, even when the path seems uncertain. Sometimes, waiting for the right moment to make a big change is the wisest choice. Think about a pair who dreams of starting a family but faces obstacles. They choose to wait, focusing on building a solid foundation first. During this time, they support each other's personal growth, celebrating small victories and learning from setbacks. This patience pays off, leading to a deeper understanding and a more profound connection. They discover that love is not about rushing to the finish line but about enjoying each moment along the way.

Growth through challenges is a common thread in these love stories. Facing difficulties together, whether financial, emotional, or otherwise, often leads to stronger relationships. For instance, when one partner struggles with a personal issue, the other stands by them, offering unwavering support. This solidarity fosters trust and intimacy, creating a partnership that thrives on mutual respect and understanding. Overcoming these challenges turns into shared triumphs, reinforcing the idea that love is about lifting each other up and growing together.

From these tales of love, we gather wisdom that's both practical and profound. Embrace change as a catalyst for growth. Instead of fearing it, see it as an opportunity to evolve and strengthen your relationship. Be patient, not just with your partner but with yourself, understanding that love takes time and effort. Persevere through hardships, knowing that each challenge is a chance to deepen your bond. Let resilience guide you, turning trials into lessons and obstacles into opportunities. And remember, love isn't about perfection; it's about the journey you take together, with all its ups and downs.

10.3 Practical Takeaways for Everyday Love

Think of love as a garden. It needs regular care, a little sunshine, and even a sprinkle of rain to bloom. Just like that garden, relationships thrive on consistent acts of love and kindness. Start with something as simple as practising daily gratitude for your partner. Take a moment each day to appreciate them, whether it's for making you laugh, being a good listener, or just being themselves. A quick "thank you" can light up their day and strengthen your bond. Regular, honest conversations are another way to keep your love healthy. Talk about everything, from your dreams to your day, and listen with an open heart. This communication builds trust and understanding, which is the foundation of any strong relationship.

Consistency in small acts is like the gentle rain that nurtures your garden. Small gestures, like leaving a thoughtful note in their bag or a reminder of something special, can mean the world. These little acts show that you're thinking of them and that they matter to you. They don't have to be grand or expensive; the thought and sincerity behind them are what count. Consider planning regular quality time together, free from distractions. Whether it's a walk in the park, a cosy movie night at home, or a shared hobby, these moments create memories and strengthen your connection. Being intentional in your actions and words makes your partner feel valued and loved.

Take a leaf from couples who manage to maintain weekly date nights despite their busy schedules. They've discovered the secret to keeping their relationship vibrant and alive. By setting aside dedicated time, they prioritise their relationship amidst life's chaos. This consistency in spending time together fosters a deeper connection and reminds them of why they fell in love in the first place. It's not always about what you do but the fact that you're doing it together. These shared experiences feed your relationship, making it richer and more rewarding. So, embrace these practical takeaways and watch your love grow into something beautiful and enduring.

Embracing Love as a Journey, Not a Destination

Love isn't a finish line you cross but an ongoing adventure filled with twists and turns. Imagine a winding road, where each new bend offers fresh scenery and experiences. That's what relationships are—a series of phases that invite growth and discovery. When you first meet someone, everything feels electric and new, but as time goes on, that initial spark evolves. It deepens into something more profound, like transitioning from the thrill of a crush to the comforting warmth of companionship. This shift isn't a sign of love fading; it's a testament to its evolution. As relationships progress, they adapt to life's changes—whether it's moving in together, starting a family, or simply growing older side by side.

The beauty of love lies in its dynamic nature. It's not static; it ebbs and flows, adapting to your needs and circumstances. Think about the beginning stages of a relationship, where everything is exciting and intense. As time passes, these feelings mature into a deep companionship. It's that moment when you realise you can sit in comfortable silence with someone, and it feels just right. Relationships also change with family dynamics. Perhaps you're blending families, or maybe you're learning to navigate life with a newborn. Each stage requires flexibility and an openness to change. Every transition, whether big or small, offers opportunities to learn and grow together. The key is to embrace these changes, welcoming the new experiences they bring.

Openness to change is what keeps relationships healthy and vibrant. It's about being flexible when life doesn't go as planned. Sometimes, it's about welcoming a new job opportunity that requires moving cities or supporting your partner through a career shift. Each experience adds layers to your connection, creating a rich tapestry of shared moments. Finding joy in the everyday journey is what makes love truly special. It's the small victories that count—like cooking a meal together without setting off the smoke alarm or managing to fit in a workout between work and kids. Celebrate these moments. They are the heartbeat of your relationship, the tiny threads that weave your life together. Embracing love as an ever-evolving process allows you to appreciate each phase for what it is, knowing that the best is always yet to come.

10.5 Cultivating Hope and Positivity in Love

Picture this: you're in a cosy room, sunlight pouring through the windows, and the air is filled with laughter. This is what focusing on the good in each other can do for a relationship. It's like watering a plant; it helps love grow stronger and more vibrant. When you make a conscious effort to see the best in your partner, it creates a positive atmosphere that nurtures both of you. This doesn't mean ignoring flaws, but rather choosing to celebrate the qualities that drew you together in the first place. It's about finding joy in the little quirks that make your partner unique and cherishing the shared moments that bring you closer.

Maintaining positivity, especially during challenging times, requires effort and intention. One powerful strategy is practising forgiveness and letting go of grudges. Holding onto past grievances is like carrying a heavy backpack; it weighs you down and prevents you from moving forward. Letting go doesn't mean forgetting or excusing hurtful behaviour, but rather freeing yourself from the burden of resentment. It's about acknowledging the hurt, discussing it openly, and then choosing to move forward together. This act of forgiveness fosters healing, paving the way for a renewed sense of trust and intimacy. It's the emotional reset button that allows you to focus on building a brighter future together.

Hope can transform relationships in remarkable ways. Imagine a couple who, after a difficult period, decides to rebuild trust. It starts with a simple conversation, an honest exchange of feelings, and a commitment to work through their issues. Slowly, hope begins to blossom. They share more, laugh more, and find themselves looking forward to the future with optimism. This renewed hope acts as a glue, binding them together and reinforcing their bond. It's a reminder that even in the darkest times, there's potential for light and growth. Hope isn't just wishful thinking; it's an active choice to believe in the possibilities and to work towards them.

Creating a supportive environment is crucial for nurturing positivity and hope. Surround yourself with friends who uplift and inspire you. These are the people who believe in love's potential and encourage you to see the good in every situation. Their optimism is contagious, and their support provides a safety net during challenging times. Whether it's a friend who listens without judgement or a family member who always has your back, these relationships create a foundation of hope that bolsters your romantic relationship. It's like building a community of love where everyone is invested in each other's happiness.

10.6 Actions Speak Louder: Love in Practice

Love, in its truest form, is shown through actions, not just words. Imagine someone promising to support you but never actually being there when you need them. It's frustrating, right? Actions are the backbone of love and trust in any relationship. When you follow through on promises, you demonstrate reliability and commitment. It's like building a sturdy bridge between your words and deeds, connecting your intentions to your partner's heart. Think of a time when someone showed up for you during a difficult moment. Whether it was a friend who brought you soup when you were sick or a partner who stood by you during a tough decision, these actions spoke volumes about their love and care.

Consider a couple who volunteers together at a local shelter every weekend. They decided to turn their shared values into concrete actions, supporting a cause they both care about. Through this joint effort, they not only helped others but also strengthened their own bond. Love in action can be as simple as helping a partner with their chores or offering a listening ear after a long day. These gestures cultivate a deeper connection, showing that love is not a passive feeling but an active choice made every day. By making these choices, you set a powerful example for those around you, illustrating how love is best expressed through deeds.

Leading by example is a profound way to inspire love in others. When you demonstrate patience and understanding, you create a ripple effect that encourages others to act lovingly. Imagine a child watching their parents express affection through kind words and supportive actions. That child learns the value of love in practice, growing up to emulate these behaviours in their own relationships. Your actions have the power to influence not just your partner but also your community. Acts of kindness, like helping a neighbour or offering a compliment, can inspire others to do the same, creating a chain reaction of love and positivity that extends far beyond your immediate circle.

10.7 Fostering a Lifelong Love Mindset

Imagine sitting with your partner, a cosy warmth enveloping you both as you talk about the future. You're not just discussing tomorrow's plans; you're envisioning a life together, crafting dreams that stretch far beyond the horizon. This is the beauty of long-term thinking in relationships. It's about seeing love as a garden that you both tend to, nurturing it with shared dreams and aspirations. Planning future goals together isn't just about ticking boxes on a list; it's an intimate dance of hopes and ambitions, aligning your paths and creating a shared vision. Maybe it's buying a home, starting a business, or simply planning the next vacation. These shared goals make each step of your journey meaningful and purposeful.

Commitment is the bedrock of sustaining love over time. It's the promise you make not just on a sunny day but during the storms, too. Remaining steadfast during tough times is the glue that holds everything together. It's about waking up every day and choosing to be there for each other, even when things get rocky. Imagine an elderly couple, hands intertwined, faces lined with years of laughter and tears. They've been through it all—financial ups and downs, health scares, family changes—but through it all, they've remained committed to each other. Their love is a testament to the power of dedication, a living example that love truly does endure all things.

To sustain lifelong love, it's crucial to regularly revisit and renew your relationship vows or promises. This doesn't mean a grand, public spectacle; it can be a quiet moment shared over morning coffee or a whispered promise before bed. These personal ceremonies are a way to reaffirm your commitment, a gentle reminder of the promises you made to each other. They give you the chance to reflect on your journey together, celebrating the milestones you've reached and the challenges you've overcome. By keeping these promises alive, you breathe new life into your relationship, ensuring it continues to grow and flourish. This mindset of nurturing a lifelong bond keeps love vibrant and enduring, like a candle that never burns out.

10.8 The Legacy of Love: Beyond Materialism

Imagine standing on a beach, watching the waves roll in. Each wave leaves its mark on the sand before retreating back into the ocean. This is much like the legacy of love—an imprint left on the hearts of those we touch, lasting long after we're gone. A legacy of love isn't about the wealth we accumulate but the cherished memories and shared experiences we create with others. It's the laughter shared around a dinner table, the stories told by a campfire, and the quiet moments of understanding shared between two people. These are the true treasures that define our lives, far surpassing any material possessions.

Building a legacy of love begins with laying a foundation of trust and kindness within your family and community. Picture a family known not for their wealth but for their generosity and service to others. Their home is a haven of kindness, where everyone is welcomed with open arms and a warm smile. Such families understand that true wealth is measured not by what you have but by what you give. They engage in activities that strengthen their bonds, like volunteering together or organising community events. These actions create ripples of love that extend beyond their immediate circle, inspiring others to act with compassion and understanding.

Consider the story of the Johnsons, a family renowned for their community service and selflessness. They didn't have much in terms of material wealth, but what they lacked in money, they made up for in heart. They spent countless weekends building homes for those in need and organising neighbourhood clean-ups. Their legacy? A community that thrived on mutual respect and support, where kindness was the currency that mattered. The Johnsons showed that the impact of love can outlast any physical structure, leaving behind a legacy that enriches lives for generations.

Now, pause to reflect on the legacy you wish to leave. Picture the lives you've touched and the memories you've created. What do you want to be remembered for? Consider writing a personal mission statement regarding love. This statement can serve as a guiding light, helping you focus on the values and actions that align with your vision of love. It can remind you to prioritise relationships over possessions, to choose kindness over wealth, and to create a legacy that celebrates the beauty of human connection. As you ponder this, imagine the waves of love you can create, leaving a lasting impact that echoes through time.

Conclusion

As we draw this journey to a close, let's pause and embrace the heart of what we've explored together. At the core of this book is a simple yet profound truth: love is more than what money can buy. It's the laughter shared over a cup of coffee, the quiet support during tough times, and the joy of simply being together. Genuine emotional connections are what truly fulfil us, far beyond the glimmer of material possessions.

Reflecting on our chapters, we've walked through the foundations of true love, where emotional intimacy and self-worth stand as pillars, much like a comforting hug on a bad day. We've ventured into the societal expectations that often cloud our judgement, reminding ourselves to break free and embrace love for what it truly is—pure and unadulterated by the world's demands. We've delved into the power of communication, not just through words but through every little gesture, understanding that sometimes a knowing glance says more than a thousand words. Then, through self-discovery, we've seen how understanding ourselves enriches our relationships. And as we navigate love in this digital age, we've learned to balance the virtual with the real, ensuring authenticity remains at the forefront. Finally, we explored the challenges that come our way and how to face them with grace, patience, and a bit of humour.

So, what's next? How about taking these ideas and sprinkling them into your own life? Start small. Maybe write a note to someone you love or plan an experience that celebrates your connection, like revisiting a favourite spot. Or, take a moment to reflect on your personal values and how they shape your relationships. The idea is to keep nurturing non-materialistic love, like tending to a garden, allowing it to grow and flourish.

Keep this book close as a companion on your journey. Let it inspire you to reflect on your values and the dynamics of your relationships. Use it as a guide to discover more about yourself and what truly matters to you. Remember, this isn't a one-time read. It's a resource for ongoing growth and self-discovery.

As you look forward, imagine a future where love in its truest form touches every corner of your life. Picture the warmth of relationships rooted in genuine care and understanding, free from the shackles of materialism. Allow hope to fill you with the promise of transformation, knowing that love—unburdened by material desires—holds the power to change both your life and the lives of those around you.

Thank you for joining me on this journey. Your willingness to explore these ideas and embrace a world where love is celebrated for its true essence is a gift. Together, we're building a community of love that values connection over consumption, authenticity over appearance, and heart over wealth.

Remember, the real wealth of life is measured in moments,

not money. Let your love be the legacy you leave behind—a testament to what truly matters. As you move forward, may you be motivated and equipped to nurture a love that transcends materialism, enriching your relationships and, ultimately, your life. Here's to a future filled with heartfelt connections and a love that endures beyond the tangible.

11

Credits & References

References

- *True Love is beyond materialism* https://www.newdelhitimes.com/true-love-is-beyond-materialism/
- *Building and Maintaining an Emotionally Wealthy Marriage* https://www.marriage.com/advice/relationship/emotionally-wealthy-marriage/
- *Building Authentic Relationships: 11 Essential Tips* https://www.marriage.com/advice/relationship/how-to-develop-authentic-relationships/
- *How Low Self-Esteem Can Impact an Intimate Relationship* https://www.psychologytoday.com/us/blog/overcoming-destructive-anger/202406/how-low-self-esteem-can-impact-an-intimate-relationship
- *The Impact of Social Media on Relationships* https://www.gottman.com/blog/the-impact-of-social-media-on-relationships/
- *Healthy Relationship Role Models* https://forums.au.reachou

t.com/t5/Community-discussions/Healthy-Relationship-Role-Models/m-p/490101

- *5 Mental Health Rewards Of Embracing Minimalism …* https://www.forbes.com/sites/traversmark/2023/06/28/5-mental-health-rewards-of-embracing-minimalism-according-to-a-psychologist/
- *The Core Values of 10 of History's Most Influential People* https://startwithvalues.com/the-core-values-of-10-of-historys-most-influential-people/
- *7 Ways to Build Emotional Intimacy with Your Partner* https://psychcentral.com/relationships/steps-to-improving-emotional-intimacy-with-your-partner
- *Importance of Nonverbal Communication in Relationships* https://www.marriage.com/advice/communication/nonverbal-communication-in-marriage/
- *Active Listening for Couples: Therapy for Stronger Bonds* https://www.mvspsychology.com.au/active-listening-for-couples-therapy-for-stronger-bonds/
- *The Importance of Vulnerability in Healthy Relationships* https://www.psychologytoday.com/us/blog/happy-healthy-relationships/202203/the-importance-of-vulnerability-in-healthy-relationships
- *The Importance of Self-Reflection in Personal Growth* https://manochikitsa.com/the-importance-of-self-reflection-in-personal-growth/
- *Empower Your Journey: 7 Key Strategies for Women to …* https://diannemdaniels.com/empower-your-journey-7-key-strategies-for-women-to-build-inner-strength/
- *22 Self-Love Exercises - How To Love Yourself \u0026 Be …* https://clevermemo.com/blog/en/self-love-exercises-how-to-love-yourself/

- *Insecurity in Relationships: Ways to Cope - Verywell Mind* https://www.verywellmind.com/coping-with-insecurity-i n-a-relationship-5207949
- *Dating and Relationships in the Digital Age* https://www.pewr esearch.org/internet/2020/05/08/dating-and-relationship s-in-the-digital-age/
- *Enhance Your Relationship with the Best Intimacy App* https://c upla.app/blog/amazing-apps-to-help-you-achieve-true- intimacy-with-your-partner/
- *How to Stop Constantly Comparing Yourself to Other ...* https://www.self.com/story/social-media-comparison -tips
- *Authentic Communication: The key to meaningful ...* https://w ww.peakgrantmaking.org/insights/authentic-communicat ion-the-key-to-meaningful-connection-and-engagemen t/
- *The Psychology of Insecurity: Understanding ...* https://mediu m.com/psych-pstuff/the-psychology-of-insecurity-under standing-the-underlying-dynamics-b3a7edf5f32f
- *How Emotional Intelligence Impacts Conflict Resolution* https://demlegaleagle.com/blog/2024/05/how-emotio nal-intelligence-impacts-conflict-resolution/
- *Setting Healthy Boundaries in Relationships* https://www.hel pguide.org/relationships/social-connection/setting-healt hy-boundaries-in-relationships
- *Friends Have More Say in Your Relationships Than You ...* https://www.psychologytoday.com/us/blog/close-encount ers/201906/friends-have-more-say-in-your-relationship s-you-think
- *5 Easy and Non-Material Ways You Can Express Your ...* https://l eiho.co.uk/blogs/all-blogs/5-easy-and-non-material-wa

ys-you-can-express-your-love-this-valentines-day?srslt
id=AfmBOopL1HBpot2EZEak1us9edOaFrjzq9LkGN8PAuc43
gWwpkzUpZlK
- *The Importance of Shared Experiences in a Relationship* https://flowjo.co/blogs/pitter-patter/the-importance-of-shared-experiences-in-a-relationship
- *53 Anniversary Date Ideas More Unique Than Just Dinner* https://www.theknot.com/content/anniversary-date-ideas
- *How Quality Time Can Transform Your Relationship* https://cupla.app/blog/how-quality-time-can-transform-your-relationship/
- *Love is Universal: 7 Romantic Traditions from Across the ...* https://www.catalystplanet.com/travel-and-social-action-stories/love-is-universal-7-romantic-traditions-from-across-the-globe
- *Strategies to Promote LGBTQ+ Inclusivity in Adult-Serving ...* https://www.acf.hhs.gov/opre/report/strategies-promote-lgbtq-inclusivity-adult-serving-healthy-marriage-and-relationship
- *Relational Models Theory* https://iep.utm.edu/r-models/
- *How Emotional Connection Can Strengthen Relationships ...* https://www.everydayhealth.com/emotional-health/how-build-emotional-connection/
- *The Inner Voice that Undermines Your Relationship - PsychAlive* https://www.psychalive.org/the-inner-voice-that-undermines-your-relationship/#:~:text=%E2%80%9CThe%20primary%20reason%20relationships%20fail,Conquer%20Your%20Critical%20Inner%20Voice.
- *Positive Self-Talk: Benefits and Techniques* https://www.healthline.com/health/positive-self-talk

- *5 Benefits of Journaling for Mental Health* https://positivepsychology.com/benefits-of-journaling/
- *Values in relationships: 7 core values for strong relationships* https://www.calm.com/blog/values-in-relationships
- *Love Beyond Materialism | Marriage* https://vocal.media/marriage/love-beyond-materialism
- *Why Patience Can Be Essential for Romantic Relationships* https://www.psychologytoday.com/us/blog/in-the-name-love/202112/why-patience-can-be-essential-romantic-relationships
- *The Little Things in Relationships That Matter the Most* https://www.verywellmind.com/the-little-things-in-relationships-that-matter-the-most-6891165

Legacy of Love: How Your Choices Impact Future ... https://drewbushman.com/2023/09/14/legacy-of-love-how-your-choices-impact-future-generations/